The
Difficult
PARENT

To Lindsey, Stephanie, and Matt
Your father was a man of great courage, kindness, and faith.

The
Difficult
PARENT

An Educator's Guide
to Handling Aggressive
Behavior

Charles M. Jaksec III

CORWIN PRESS
A Sage Publications Company
Thousand Oaks, California

For information:

Corwin Press
A Sage Publications Company
2455 Teller Road
Thousand Oaks, California 91320
www.corwinpress.com

Sage Publications Ltd.
1 Oliver's Yard
55 City Road
London EC1Y 1SP
United Kingdom

Sage Publications India Pvt. Ltd.
B-42, Panchsheel Enclave
Post Box 4109
New Delhi 110 017 India

Printed in the United States of America

Library of Congress Cataloging-in-Publication Data

Jaksec, Charles M.
The difficult parent: An educator's guide to handling aggressive behavior / Charles M. Jaksec III.
    p. cm.
Includes bibliographical references and index.
ISBN 0-7619-8898-X (cloth)
ISBN 0-7619-8899-8 (pbk.)
    1. Parent-teacher relationships—Handbooks, manuals, etc. 2. Aggressiveness—Prevention—Handbooks, manuals, etc. 3. Communication in education—Handbooks, manuals, etc. I. Title
LC226.J35 2005
371.103—dc22   2004007965

This book is printed on acid-free paper.

06   07   08   09   10   9   8   7   6   5   4   3   2

Acquisitions Editor:	Robert D. Clouse
Editorial Assistant:	Jingle Vea
Production Editor:	Denise Santoyo
Copy Editor:	Liann Lech
Typesetter:	C&M Digitals (P) Ltd.
Indexer:	Kathy Paparchontis
Cover Designer:	Tracy E. Miller
Graphic Designer:	Anthony Paular

Contents

Acknowledgments

I would like to acknowledge the many school personnel who took the time to provide their input and insights. Without them, this effort would not have been possible. Also, Susan Jaksec provided much appreciated technical assistance. I would like to thank Robb Clouse at Corwin Press for interest in this project. His advice was invaluable. My mentor in the field of school social work is Kitty Van Zile. I will always appreciate her guidance and support.

My wife Samantha, daughter Jordan, and son Michael are sources of strength for me. I love our family! Finally, as always, thank you Jesus, Mary, Joseph, and Jude for always being there for me.

In addition, Corwin Press gratefully acknowledges the contributions of the following people:

Susan Whitefield
Principal, Righetti High School
Santa Maria, CA

Chris D. Funk
Principal, Abraham Lincoln High School
San Jose, CA

Ken James
Principal, Highland High School
Gilbert, AZ

Diane Rudolph
Principal, Perryville Middle School
Perryville, MD

Harold Bower
Principal, Grand Rapids Elementary School
Grand Rapids, OH

Jane Howerter
Principal, Lost Creek Elementary School
Columbus, NE

Craig C. Browne
Principal, Harold Wilson Middle School
Newark, NJ

Joseph Staub
Resource Specialist Teacher
Thomas Starr King Middle School
Los Angeles, CA

Edward Chevallier
Principal, Blalack Middle School
Carrollton, TX

Susan M. Nakaba
Associate Principal
Palos Verdes High School
Rolling Hills Estates, CA

Patti Kinney
Principal, Talent Middle School
Ashland, OR

Rosemarie Young
Principal, NAESP President-Elect
Watson Lane Elementary School
Louisville, KY

Regina Birdsell
Principal, Academy Elementary School
Madison, CT

Gloria Kumagai
Principal, Museum Magnet Elementary School
Golden Valley, MN

About the Author

 **Charles M. Jaksec III** is a school social worker with the Hillsborough County School District in Tampa, Florida. He is also a member of the district's Crisis Intervention Team. Jaksec received his undergraduate degree in social work from Slippery Rock University of Pennsylvania, where he also received a master's degree in counseling services. At the University of South Florida, he received his EdS in counselor education and a PhD in curriculum and instruction. He has authored journal and magazine articles on the topic of parental aggression and is the author of the book, *The Confrontational Parent: A Practical Guide for School Leaders.* He speaks nationally on the topic of parental aggression.

Jaksec resides in Tampa, Florida, with his wife, Samantha, who is an independent reading consultant, and their children, Jordan and Michael.

Introduction

During the past several years, I've engaged in research that examined the issue of parental aggression toward school administrators. This unique, albeit obscure, educational issue appealed to me because at the time, little, if any, research existed on the topic. The results of my research led me to author the book, *The Confrontational Parent: A Practical Guide for School Leaders.* In addition to containing the results of my research, the book also included anecdotes from school administrators throughout the country on the topic of parental aggression.

I discovered that school leaders were undoubtedly experiencing occurrences of parental aggression, and these same school administrators also wanted their school districts to direct attention toward this issue. As a result of these findings, I decided to create a simple yet effective tool that might assist school administrators during their encounters with aggressive parents. Subsequently, the RAID Approach was born. Although described briefly in my first book, the RAID Approach will now form the foundation of this book, *The Difficult Parent: An Educator's Guide to Handling Aggressive Behavior.* In this effort, however, the application of the RAID Approach will not be featured for use by school administrators exclusively but also by other school personnel, including teachers, counselors, social workers, school psychologists, school nurses, and office personnel. I decided to expand the RAID Approach for use by non-administrative school personnel because, while conducting my research, many of these staff members asked, "Why couldn't we also use the RAID Approach?" In addition, as the result of positive feedback from my first book, I decided that input and anecdotes from school personnel around the country would again be appealing to the reader. Subsequently, *The Difficult Parent* contains chapters that include scenarios in which many types of school personnel can easily observe the workings of the RAID Approach. These scenarios will

1

appear somewhat familiar to traditional educators because they are based on actual, day-to-day experiences of educators.

The Difficult Parent was written with educational practitioners in mind. Wordy, complicated formulas and cookbook-type instructions are nonexistent. This book simply requires that the reader be familiar with the importance of communication and the difficulties that aggressive individuals may present.

The Difficult Parent is a three-part book. Part 1 discusses the issue of parental aggression as it pertains to educators. Part 2 focuses on an in-depth examination of the RAID Approach and its mechanics. Part 3 discusses the actual implementation of the RAID Approach.

Throughout this book, I will make references to parents who display aggressive or confrontational behavior toward school personnel. This may seem like a negative view of parents and guardians. That being said, it's important to explain that these parents are described for the purposes of this book. Aggressive parents were simply the focus of my research, and they comprise only a small fraction of the parents who interact with school personnel on a day-to-day basis. It goes without saying that the majority of parents are truly a pleasure to work with. Parents remain a vital source of support for school personnel and are often counted on to provide services too extensive to list here. As a social worker, my job is to interact with parents with the hope of overcoming obstacles that may negatively affect their child's school performance. Even in these difficult situations, I can recall few parents who actually presented problems to the extent that communication was impossible.

Nonetheless, certain parents unfortunately exhibit behaviors that make their interactions with school personnel problematic. These are the individuals whom this book addresses. Although the techniques described here could certainly be adapted for use with other aggressive individuals, I dedicated my efforts to the examination of a specific population: parents.

PART I

Parental Aggression Toward School Personnel

CHAPTER ONE

A Genuine Concern for School Personnel

ARE CONFRONTATIONAL PARENTS A PERTINENT ISSUE?

I could safely presume that the individuals who consider reading this book have at least thought of the difficulties that a confrontational parent presents. To go a step further, I could also make two assumptions. First, most of these readers have actually encountered a confrontational or aggressive parent, and second, very few of these encounters resulted in pleasant farewells between the staff member and the parent.

One question immediately arises: "How pertinent is the issue of school personnel and their encounters with confrontational parents?" I think I can best answer this question by first defining the word "pertinence" as the degree to which something affects or is important to an individual. Answering the question of "pertinence" using this definition allows me to reason that parental confrontation really is an important issue to many types of school personnel. This issue is made all the more obvious when you realize that any confrontation is significant because it alters the behavior of the staff member in his or her efforts to address the issues of the aggressive parent.

Confrontation is a powerful tool because, when used properly, it allows another individual to consider the effects of his or her behavior. Unfortunately, as many educators discover, confrontation with an overly aggressive parent usually produces little in the way of positive results. Parental aggression also comes in many forms, including physical or verbal. In addition, threats such as the invasion of personal space or gestures made in an effort to intimidate also constitute types of aggression.

Yes, confrontational parents need to be addressed. For any type of school personnel, interactions with parents who display aggressive or confrontational behavior rarely occur without repercussion. Whether these interactions result in an inconvenient disruption of a workday or even a threat to the employee's safety, parental aggression is a problem not to be ignored.

How Often Does Parental Aggression Occur?

When I first considered conducting research on the topic of parental aggression, the issue of frequency was the first question I wanted to answer. "How often were educators actually being confronted by aggressive parents?" Before I answer this question, it is important to explain—and emphasize—that the type of aggression being perpetrated by the parents largely determined the frequency of aggression. For example, concerning the specific issue of verbal aggression toward school administrators, I asked administrators to respond to the School Administrator Parent Aggression Survey (SAPAS) (Jaksec, 2003). Six hundred sixty-nine surveys were sent to school administrators (mostly principals and assistant principals) in Florida's 67 school districts. Florida can be generalized to other states because its districts adequately comprise suburban, rural, and urban schools throughout the nation. Socioeconomically, school districts in Florida are also well represented. I discovered that

- 60% of the administrators had profanity or shouting directed at them by parents on at least two occasions during the school year.
- 70% of the administrators had false accusations leveled against them by parents during the school year.
- 79% of the school administrators—on three or more occasions—reported receiving parental threats to contact "other authorities," that is, attorneys, school board, and so on.

Parental aggression, specifically verbal aggression, does occur, and more often than I originally suspected.

While I was conducting this research on parental aggression, colleagues from around the country sent me headlines involving stories of confrontational interactions with parents. I recall one episode that involved a superintendent in California who was actually handcuffed by two parents, placed under citizen's arrest, and taken away in their car, all while being videotaped by the mother. Fortunately, 10 miles later, a sheriff's deputy stopped the car and freed the superintendent. The reason for the parents' actions? The couple, long dissatisfied with district policy, sent a 15-page letter accusing school officials of giving sexually explicit materials to students. After the couple imposed a deadline to resolve their concern (which was not met), they accosted the superintendent.

In another incident, a 31-year teaching veteran in Boston was attacked by a mother who objected to discipline issues regarding her son. The teacher suffered a seizure and a broken cheekbone that required surgery. In addition, the teacher's eye remained dilated and glaucoma may have resulted. Dental surgery was also considered.

It is easy to read these sensational media headlines and assume that "it only happens to someone else," but aggression, even perpetrated by parents, can occur anywhere and at any time. Aggression also presents itself in not-so-newsworthy forms. For instance, a parent might threaten an administrator with legal action because he or she feels negligence was exhibited during a field trip, a physical education teacher might be confronted on the playground by a parent whose child has reported being bullied by a peer, or a school social worker might have profanity directed toward him or her by a parent during a conference. These situations can understandably affect the way school personnel function, and they occur more frequently than you think.

DO EMPLOYEES HAVE TO TOLERATE PARENTAL AGGRESSION?

We've established that some forms of parental aggression and confrontations occur quite frequently. Now, the question emerges, "Do I have to tolerate it?" In any circumstance, aggression from a student is difficult to accept for school personnel. An aggressive act by a parent or guardian remains an even more difficult pill to swallow. Understandably, educators expect that parents are mature adults who, for all intents and purposes, know better than to resort to nonconstructive, confrontational behavior. Alas, this is not always the case.

Certainly, no one actually tells school personnel that abuse is acceptable. In fact, there has been an increase in civility policies in our nation's school districts. These policies emphasize that any threatening behaviors—on the part of any party, including school personnel—will not be tolerated and are sometimes punishable. Illogically, school personnel continue to encounter aggressive parents who, for a variety of reasons to be discussed in this chapter, challenge school employees. Regrettably, during these interactions, communication can erode so that little is accomplished.

Who are the real "losers" as the result of these encounters? Quite possibly the students, because, in all likelihood, they will learn the same negative styles of communication as their parents. The parents, though, also suffer because their poor manner of communication might interfere or delay a solution to the problem facing their own child. In addition, the educators lose because these turbulent encounters have a cumulative effect, which might possibly affect their performance.

Are school personnel paid enough to put up with confrontational parents or their acts of aggression? No way! However, I'm also aware that of the countless numbers of school employees whom I have interviewed and with whom I have corresponded through the years, very few have encountered a problematic parent and, as a result, said "goodbye" to the field of education. Are the personnel who have encountered such a parent frustrated and angry? Of course they are, and understandably so. However, I believe that if an effective, yet simple manner of dealing with these parents were available for school personnel, their jobs could be made much easier and less aggravating.

COULD PARENTAL AGGRESSION AFFECT ME?

Could a confrontational or overly aggressive parent affect any type of school personnel? I would undoubtedly answer yes. I could dedicate several chapters to comments made to me by school administrators who, in the past, had the misfortune of encountering hostile parents. Many of these encounters produced uneasy feelings and even physical reactions that genuinely affected the way the staff members functioned. I have heard personnel discuss various ailments, including muscle tension, fatigue, hypertension, teeth grinding, and an assortment of other medically related issues that were the direct result of these turbulent encounters. School personnel have also explained to me that they have suffered from depression, anxiousness, sleeplessness, or a host of other ailments that they directly attributed to difficulties with hostile parents. Logically, not all school personnel are affected to the same degree; however, I have observed that very few educators emerged physically or emotionally unscathed from unpleasant encounters with parents.

Turbulent encounters also seem to produce a level of response that is commensurate with the staff member's level of experience. The effects of parent hostility could possibly be more devastating to a staff member with little experience in contrast to an employee with vast experience. It should be emphasized, however, that seasoned school personnel are not immune to the effects of aggression because of their experience, and ramifications, some serious, remain for both inexperienced and experienced school personnel.

Experienced professionals have told me of their intention to change career fields, transfer schools, or change positions in order to avoid conflicts with parents. I find this very unfortunate because the movement of these competent professionals ultimately places the student at a disadvantage. Fortunately, the great majority of educational personnel who discuss with me their interactions with aggressive parents chose to remain in the field of education. It is important to remember that the choice to remain does not indicate that these encounters do not take their toll on the educator in a variety of ways.

WHY DOES THE TOPIC OF PARENTAL AGGRESSION SEEM OBSCURE?

Discussions regarding aggression within our nation's schools usually involve student-perpetrated violence toward staff or classmates. The amount of information and research available regarding this type of aggression is seemingly limitless, and this topic presents itself continuously. The emphasis on student-perpetrated aggression has also piqued nationwide interest on the topic. Subsequently, this has resulted in a decline of violent acts in our schools.

In contrast, the topic of parental aggression toward school employees does not receive nearly the same amount of exposure.

This is evident by the lack of research and literature on the topic. Unquestionably, the topic of parental aggression toward school personnel is somewhat obscure. But why? I find three possible reasons for this uniqueness: responsibility, resiliency, and a lack of awareness.

Responsibility

One reason for the uniqueness of the topic of parental aggression is the mind-set that school personnel are actually responsible or expected to deal with the parent regardless of the parent's disposition. If this mind-set is prevalent—and it may, in fact, be—it is unfortunate and dangerous. Although educators should be responsive to parent needs and requests, they do not have the same responsibility if the behavior of these parents becomes hostile or aggressive.

Resiliency

The one word that most accurately describes most educators is "resilient." Whether it is the math teacher who determinedly attempts to teach fractions to a distracted student; the school social worker who tirelessly tries to build rapport with a detached parent; or the front-office worker who addresses myriad concerns, requests, or complaints on a daily basis, resiliency at most schools is on display 5 days per week. One problem with this resiliency is the educator's occasional failure to expose or report incidences of parental aggression. The longer the actions of an aggressive parent go unaddressed, the longer that parent is free to interact aggressively with other school personnel.

Lack of Awareness

Parental aggression remains a somewhat obscure issue because it is conceivable that educators may be unaware of the effects of these turbulent encounters. Perhaps educators consider the emotional or physical effects from parent aggression to be similar to the effects of any other type of conflict (i.e., a conflict with a student or an argument with a colleague). Subsequently, incidences involving aggressive parents are not reported by school personnel. Although it is not possible to measure the effects of different types of conflict, educators should be aware of the ramifications of these altercations.

If educators rethink their responsibility to interact with aggressive parents, acknowledge their resiliency, and become aware of the ramifications of interacting with volatile parents, the issue of parental aggression might transform a very obscure issue into an important concern.

What Makes Parental Aggression a Unique Issue?

When we discuss parental aggression toward school employees, we tend to think about this topic as part of the larger issue of school violence. Although this is true, parental aggression is also a unique issue for several reasons.

It's Your Kid But It's Our Student

When a hostile parent is encountered, chances are, the problem has something to do with his or her child. Ironically, this same child attends your school. Obviously, the parent sees nothing more important than the welfare of his or her child. Similarly, school personnel are in the position to assist, not hinder, the student. Unfortunately, staff members and parents often find themselves at odds for any number of reasons, and as unnecessary as these conflicts may be, they do occur. Much like a divorce, the child is placed in the middle of the conflict. To the credit of most educators, I have met few individuals who let their view of the parent taint their relationship with the child. However, it remains a difficult challenge for staff members to maintain a favorable attitude toward a family when one or both of the parents prove to be aggressive or confrontational.

The Volatility of the Issue

Optimally, parents and school personnel work as partners in order to provide the academic environment and support necessary for student success. Usually, this arrangement is successful. When disagreements do occur, the educator discovers that few issues create more emotion than a parent who believes that his or her child has been wronged in some way by someone or something at the school. Unfortunately, by the time parents make their problems or demands known, they occasionally become so emotional that school personnel are unprepared in their attempts to address the parents' problem. These situations can quickly deteriorate to the point where little, if anything, is accomplished.

Parent aggression occurs at every level within a school district. From the front office to the superintendent's office, parent aggression can emerge and pose many problems for everyone involved. As we will see later in this book, this extensive problem often necessitates a multidisciplined approach by school personnel.

Repercussions for the Educator

Parental aggression is also unique because volatile parents are capable of exercising options that cause legitimate concern and stress for school personnel. Most educators have encountered a parent who unnecessarily chose to take an unresolved problem or conflict to the next level of administration. Other parents may have even threatened school board or legal action. Although some educators refuse to take these threats seriously, others do, and so these parental options are perceived as a threat to the educators' professional standing. Many employees have "sweated out" a parent's decision to move a complaint, whether warranted or unwarranted, to the next level in an effort to receive satisfaction. The impending repercussions are very stressful to these professionals, but nonetheless, these options remain at the parent's disposal.

An All-Encompassing Problem

If you briefly recall an instance in which a parent became aggressive toward a school employee, it will become immediately obvious that the situation involved several other types of school personnel. For instance, front-office personnel inform a principal of the arrival of an irate parent. The principal initially summons the assistant principal and asks if he or she is aware of any previous violent behaviors on the parent's part. Upon hearing that the parent has a history of violence, the school resource officer is asked to remain near the conference room.

This situation involved four types of people: front-office personnel, principal, assistant principal, and school resource officer. Luckily, this situation was responded to by personnel who just happened to be available when school personnel required their services. In subsequent chapters, more complicated scenarios will be presented that illustrate the actions of various types of school personnel when they are confronted with aggressive or hostile parents. Parent aggression is truly unique in that it involves many types of school personnel.

What follows are discussion questions that relate to school personnel interactions with aggressive or confrontational parents. Discussion questions will also be included at the conclusion of each subsequent chapter. These questions are intended to help the reader apply the information from each chapter to his or her own experiences.

QUESTIONS FOR DISCUSSION

1. In the past 2 years, how many times have you encountered an aggressive or confrontational parent? Try to recall the reasons for the parent's disposition and behavior. Do you feel he or she was justified?

2. Do you know a colleague who has been physically or psychologically affected by an encounter with an aggressive parent? Have you noted a specific type of staff member that may be more prone to parental aggression than other types of personnel?

3. Is your school district aware of the issue of parental aggression? If so, what has been done to address this issue? In your opinion, could more attention be directed toward it?

CHAPTER TWO

The Reactive Nature of Education

I f I were asked, "What word most accurately describes our society?" I would probably respond "reactive." I could simply point to the increased security at our airports and establishment of a homeland security agency as the result of the September 11, 2001, attacks. We certainly reacted to this tragedy, but unfortunately, much less was done along these lines prior to the attacks. Similarly, in our nation's schools, support personnel occasionally engage in crisis intervention services in an effort to return the school to its normal state of precrisis functioning. Again, intervention is rendered only after the crisis has occurred, not prior to it.

I think it is natural to react immediately after a turbulent event; however, does this reactive approach best serve us as educators? By waiting for a crisis to occur, we may be working at a distinct disadvantage. Reactivity ensures one thing—that damage has been done—and the onus is placed on the interventionist to make a traumatic situation better, and as soon as possible. For instance, as the war in Iraq grew into a real possibility in 2002, I could not help but note the hesitance of our nation's schools to gradually but gently expose students to the possibility of war and the possible psychological effects that would result. Of course, not every school population was affected as the war approached, but many schools did contain students who were affected or maybe could have benefited from some form of intervention prior to the start of the war.

As employees in the field of education, you may, at one time or another, have been placed in a situation that resulted from this "reactive" approach. For instance, try to recall an encounter with a parent who may have been very irritated, confrontational, or just plain angry. By the time you actually sat down to a conference or meeting to address the issue at hand, you likely found yourself in a somewhat defensive position, maybe even attempting to calm the irate parent. You were in the unenviable position of reacting to the parent's behavior rather than attempting to achieve a solution to the parent's problem. Ironically, the parent's own child was more often than not the reason you were interacting with the parent in the first place!

In direct contrast to this reactive approach is a proactive or preventive approach toward dealing with a crisis or turbulent situation. During my years as a district crisis intervention counselor, I have become quite familiar with an Israeli model of crisis intervention that focuses on "primary prevention." This model allows Israeli students to address their fears about war and possible terrorist attacks prior to the actual event. It is intended that when and if the attack actually transpires, students will be more capable of handling the psychological effects of the event. At this point you may ask, "How does Israeli crisis intervention apply to my dealings with volatile parents?" This could best be answered by first emphasizing that school personnel are, of course, not at war with parents. In fact, the great majority of parents are truly supportive of educators and school employees. That being said, it can be reasoned that waiting for a confrontation to occur at a meeting or conference is actually akin to the reactive approach mentioned earlier. Interventions with volatile parents need to begin before the meeting is conducted. This is an ominous task, to say the least. Simply, a preemptive approach must be implemented in order to avoid unnecessary difficulties later in the meeting with the parent. This now sounds much like the Israeli model.

Theo S. is a guidance counselor in a large Florida middle school. A veteran of more than 15 years of guidance experience, she explains that

> There have been several instances that I have interacted with hostile parents. Several of these incidences involved the handling of discipline issues involving their children. In each of these occurrences, I was taken aback because of the nature of their accusations and the abrupt shift from my previous interactions

with them. The parents made accusatory remarks toward school personnel, i.e., being unfair. They also threatened legal action. I noticed that during these interactions, the parents usually raised their voices and did not want to listen to any other point of view or explanation. Although I have tried to placate parents and offer rational explanations for the events in question, parents who are seemingly out of control have trouble listening to reason. I maintain that the best way to deal with parental issues is to remain calm and not take the attack personally; a preventative approach might just help.

The Effects of Reactivity

By utilizing a preventive or preemptive approach toward confrontational or aggressive parents, staff members can greatly diminish the intensity of the encounter or maybe even avoid the encounter altogether. The effect of remaining in a reactive posture is debilitating in the sense that staff members are constantly defending their view or stance on the issue or problem at hand. "Waiting for the shoe to drop" is not a pleasant feeling for an educator; it is probably an accurate feeling, however, if the parent's aggressiveness is dictating the course of the meeting.

Beth L. is a secretary at a large middle school in Florida. She described an incident in which a parent arrived on campus demanding to see the assistant principal.

While awaiting the administrator in the front office, the parent began speaking to me in a very hostile tone. She loudly stated that the assistant principal was discriminating against her child. Several times, I asked the parent to calm down, however, she only became more agitated. I then informed the parent that if she did not calm down, I would have no other recourse than to call for assistance. Unfortunately, the parent continued talking in a loud, rude manner. I attempted to use the walkie-talkie to contact an administrator, however, no one was available. Finally, I walked down the hall and asked the school resource officer to assist me. By that time, administrators arrived and along with the school resource officer escorted the belligerent parent off campus.

When I asked Beth her opinion of her campus's method of addressing hostile parents, she felt that her school traditionally did an excellent job with these types of parents. The secretary continued to explain, however, that although this tense situation resolved itself, she was indeed exposed to a very volatile individual. I asked Beth, "What would have happened if the school resource officer had not been available?" She pondered the question and was uneasy at the thought of this possibility. Beth also admitted that her school's approach was "defensive" in nature, reacting to the actions of hostile individuals, such as the parent she encountered. For Beth, this realization was admittedly unsettling, yet this defensive posture is found in most of our nation's schools. Unfortunately, seldom does a preemptive or proactive plan exist in regard to hostile parents. The main reason for a failure to employ more preemptive stances has simply been the absence of approaches that allow school personnel to take control of these situations.

Is a Proactive Approach Necessary?

When pondering the question of necessity regarding the establishment of approaches for dealing with aggressive parents, I discovered that 71% of the respondents indicated that parental aggression was an issue that required more attention by their school districts. I also found that 76% of the respondents agreed or strongly agreed that their colleagues voiced their concern regarding parental aggression. In addition, 42% of the educators agreed or strongly agreed that they altered their approaches with parents because of previous encounters with hostile parents. Finally, 58% of the surveys indicated that the respondents either disagreed or strongly disagreed that they would not conduct a meeting with a parent who was considered hostile (Jaksec, 2003). These facts considered, a proactive approach toward the issue of parental aggression might indeed be necessary.

Why Does This Feel Funny?

Although a proactive approach—in lieu of a reactive approach— might be considered by some educators, the fact remains that a proactive approach toward volatile individuals is quite different from what educators are accustomed to. Taking the initiative often takes some getting used to. To make a point, let's revisit the area of crisis intervention. The thought of addressing the issue of death before it actually occurs is, for the most part, distasteful, at least in the United States. Similarly, the thought of heading off or preempting a confrontation with an aggressive parent—although a wise option— may understandably produce a degree of discomfort. But why? I think that these uneasy feelings could be related to the lack of structure or established approaches available to educators regarding the handling of confrontational parents. As in the area of crisis intervention, a fixed approach or system of involvement can go a long way toward increasing the confidence of educators when they find themselves interacting with aggressive parents. Maybe if staff members were well versed and familiar in new, preemptive approaches, the entire process wouldn't feel so "funny."

WHY DO PARENTS BECOME HOSTILE?

If there were only one or two reasons why parents became hostile or aggressive, it is likely that a solution or effective response could be attained easily. Unfortunately, this is not the case, and educators continue to wonder why parent hostility rears itself in our schools. Several factors are recognized as main contributors to parental aggression (Jaksec, 2003). These factors include financial stress, patterns of family violence, unstable family environments, previous negative school experiences, school personnel attitudes, a parent's mental instability, or even a fear that he or she is actually losing control of his or her child. All of these variables can result in hostility being directed toward school personnel. I would like to identify several additional, but not commonly identified, factors that might generate parental aggression.

Lack of Familiarity

As a school social worker, I am fully aware of the difficulties that result from a parent's refusal to become actively involved in his or her child's school endeavors. In a sense, these parents have alienated themselves from the school and remain unfamiliar with school personnel. When a problem or issue inevitably arises, the parent has little familiarity with these staff members. This lack of familiarity could become problematic because a highly emotional issue would be in the eyes of the parent, addressed by a "stranger." In contrast, parents who take a strong interest in their child's education tend to be familiar with school personnel who are involved with their child. By becoming familiar with school personnel, the parent becomes aware of the personalities, expectations, and standards of these individuals. This applies whether the employee is the child's principal, teacher, guidance counselor, and so on. The advantages of this familiarity also benefit school personnel because they, too, begin to know the parent's traits or characteristics. Realistically, it could also be presumed that familiarity lessens the intensity of interactions between parents and school personnel when problems do emerge.

Inaccurate Perceptions of School Personnel

It is a daunting challenge to educate our nation's children to function in an ever-changing world. As a result, the subsequent restructuring of our nation's schools will ensure that parents will always disagree occasionally with issues related to this change.

Brandt (1998) concludes that

Americans are obsessed with the basics. They can't understand why schools seemingly refuse to put "first things first" when everyone agrees basic skills are absolutely essential. . . . Most people are doubtful about practices—such as detracking, holistic reading, writing, and early use of the calculator—that experts advocate. And they reveal a striking difference in what people mean by standards. While educator groups have been developing long lists of delicately worded aspirations, ordinary people just think kids should not be promoted if they can't do the work at their current grade level. (p. 2)

The aforementioned quote emphasizes the point that parents do not always view educators as proceeding in ways that benefit their children. Interestingly, parents view themselves as demanding customers. The results of a survey conducted by the Education Commission of the United States (1966) indicated that people desire change, but disagreement exists regarding how much and what type of change. As a result, parents are often skeptical of education and possibly the intentions of educators. Brandt (1998) explains that a clue to this skepticism is the discovery that parents depend on teachers more than any other source of information regarding educational matters. Intriguingly, this does not include the child's *school* teacher, but rather their teacher in clubs or churches. According to Brandt, credibility does not exist between progressive education and parents alone, but also between advocates of traditional ways and new ways, both outside and within the profession.

Parents continue to be less trusting of institutions, including government. Also, public schools are often the target of negative media attention, and certain groups exploit situations of questionable actions of educators. As a result, parents view school personnel inaccurately, and these misperceptions certainly affect subsequent interaction with these professionals. Compounding these concerns are traditional parent complaints that educators do not hear their needs. Parents may also perceive school employees (especially administrators) as intimidating (Jaksec, 2003). Jane Lindle (1989) discovered that whereas educators felt that parents wanted them to act professional and businesslike, the parents desired the opposite. At all socioeconomic levels, parents complained of principals and teachers being condescending or patronizing. The parents were fond of educators who possessed a "personal touch." Lindle notes that parents desire that educators be "real." An educator's attitude and personal characteristics were also considered paramount.

Lack of Civility Policies

In my opinion, one of the main reasons that parents act out on school campuses is the absence of policies that identify what these individuals can or can't do on campus. To a degree, civility policies regulate behavior within an academic setting. After interacting in an aggressive or hostile manner, these individuals frequently are simply escorted off campus with little regard to the severity of their behaviors. Unfortunately, little or no repercussions result from these behaviors. Although civility policies are merely written statements, sometimes they do prove effective in delineating rules or expectations. In all likelihood, aggressive acts toward school personnel will continue, but civility policies will hopefully "make a dent" in aggressive acts toward school personnel. Amazingly, civility policies do not exist in many of our nation's schools. This is unfortunate, because the effort to establish such policies is minimal and their benefit is substantial. The avoidance of even one volatile encounter makes a civility policy worthwhile.

These three overlooked factors can dramatically affect parental behavior on most school campuses. It is understandable that a parent's lack of understanding regarding school personnel, his or her misperception of school personnel, and the absence of behavioral guidelines all strongly contribute to increasing the chances of volatile parental encounters with school personnel.

QUESTIONS FOR DISCUSSION

1. Do you tend to be more reactive or proactive in your approach to turbulent situations? Is there a reason for this tendency?

2. In your opinion, what are the three main reasons why parents become aggressive toward school personnel?

3. Is there a code of conduct or civility statement visible in your school? If not, do you feel that this option would be beneficial for school personnel?

CHAPTER THREE

Confrontational Parents and Your Colleagues

I commented earlier that the vast majority of educators have probably experienced at least one negative encounter with a parent or guardian. During my numerous interviews and discussions with school employees, I rarely, if ever, meet a professional who can't share a "doozy" of a story involving a particularly hostile parent. During these discussions, I've been informed of a variety of techniques and suggestions for handling parents who became at odds with school personnel for any reason. In my opinion, these stories ranged from what I considered amusing to what I considered scary. I've also observed that tolerance toward aggressive parents ranged from those professionals with "long fuses" to those with very little patience. Fortunately, few school employees failed to take the issue of parental aggression seriously.

Most of these turbulent interactions will result in agreed-upon solutions to the issue or problem at hand. However, hostile or uncivil behavior could also be directed toward any type of school personnel, from a superintendent to office personnel.

These interactions can result in school-level ramifications. It's conceivable that staff productivity might be negatively affected, and school climate and morale might also deteriorate if school personnel do not feel safe.

Various scenarios will illustrate how parents can come into conflict with school personnel. I have included professionals who traditionally comprise the faculties at most of our nation's campuses. Various types of personnel were included in an attempt to demonstrate the specific challenges that may be unique for individuals in their specific professions (i.e., teaching, nursing, social work, etc.). Let's examine what specific areas of parental aggression pose unique difficulties for professions within the field of education.

SCHOOL ADMINISTRATORS

Among all school personnel, administrators find themselves in the most vulnerable position in regard to parent aggression. There are several reasons for this. First, although school leaders allow for input from colleagues and parents, they make the final decision in regard to matters within their schools. Administrators also maintain some level of involvement in numerous school activities and responsibilities. This obviously increases the chances of problems emerging and subsequent interactions with parents who may demand that the administrator remedy the problem to their satisfaction. Without a doubt, the seemingly omnipresent school administrator avails him- or herself to a wide range of difficulties that sometimes result in encounters with parents who may be aggressive.

As discussed in Chapter 1, examples of aggression perpetrated by parents may include verbal threats, accusations, intimidation, or physical attacks (Jaksec, 2003). Parents also possess the leverage to contact attorneys or school board members if they are dissatisfied with an administrative decision. In addition, school administrators have voiced their concerns that dissatisfied or aggressive parents occasionally go over their heads to higher-level administrators in an effort to receive satisfaction. School leaders have voiced concern that a parent's decision to take his or her complaint to the next level will reflect poorly on them. One administrator was concerned that these instances could hurt his chances of vertical mobility within his school district because he was not remedying these problems at the school level.

Although school administrators may encounter various forms of parent aggression, they often possess several characteristics that enable them to adequately address hostile behavior. For instance, most school leaders have significant years of experience, which were required for them to attain the position. This experience serves the administrator well because it permits exposure to various personality types. In addition, although all school personnel should be respected by parents (and vice versa), one would suppose that respect would be displayed particularly toward school leaders because of their position or standing within the school. Generally, this is true, but far too frequently, school administrators continue to find themselves the focal point of parental aggression.

TEACHERS

While I conducted my studies on the topic of confrontational parents, I explored techniques or approaches that might assist school administrators when interacting with these individuals. During this period, I was approached by a teacher who was quite perturbed. She asked why I hadn't addressed the issue of parental aggression toward classroom teachers. I thought about her inquiry and came to the conclusion that teachers probably have more contacts with parents throughout the school year than any other type of school personnel. Whether via scheduled conferences, telephone contacts, or the day-to-day progress of their students, teachers seem to be in constant communication with parents.

This frequency of contact would logically increase the likelihood of a turbulent encounter. Teachers have told me about numerous instances of parents threatening, accusing, or intimidating them. I recall a certain teacher who met a parent on conference night. The teacher expressed to me her feelings of fear and helplessness as the parent became hostile and there were no other personnel in her classroom's vicinity. Teachers occasionally are the recipients of parental aggression for a variety of reasons. Foremost could be the parents' frustration that their child has not achieved an expected level of competence in the teacher's class. Unfairly, the teacher is perceived as being the ultimate reason for the child's failure.

Additional stress can result from the teacher's concern that the dissatisfied parent will take his or her issue to the administrative level. This specific parental option is a concern for some teachers, who think that their actions, even if justified, will be questioned by their superiors if a parent complains. Understandably, teachers, like other school personnel, are affected by attacks against their professionalism, knowledge, and competence. Parents can also be unaware of the depth of student-teacher relationships, because few other types of school personnel have contact with students on a daily basis as teachers do. A healthy parent-teacher relationship is essential because it helps to improve the student's classroom performance. Conversely, if the parent-teacher relationship is volatile, the student's success could be compromised.

Guidance Counselors

Whereas teachers and students share the most consistent day-to-day contact, guidance counselors share a different type of relationship with students—this, due to the fact that students seek the services of the guidance counselors in an attempt to alleviate some type of academic or interpersonal difficulty. As any counselor is aware, these contacts may, at times, be intense. Student difficulties are often related to issues at home, and, subsequently, this brings the counselor in direct contact with a student's parents. As the counselor contacts the parent to inform him or her of the issue at hand, the sensitivity of the matter may produce forms of defensiveness, aggression, or hostility from the parent. The parent may also react out of frustration if the issue has affected the family for a significant amount of time. In addition, some guidance counselors are responsible for contacting child protection agencies and thus face the uncertainty of parental retribution if abuse or neglect allegations have been made against parents.

Guidance counselors are prone to the same types of parental aggression as their colleagues. They occasionally experience verbal aggression, physical threats, and allegations as they attempt to interact with parents under intense circumstances. Another distinction between guidance counselors and other school personnel is the frequency of contact with parents. Similar to teachers, counselors are in frequent contact with parents regarding a student's academic or behavior concerns. This rate of occurrence could lend itself to an increase in turbulent encounters. Fortunately, most guidance counselors are well versed in interpersonal techniques acquired during their experience and formal education. This interpersonal proficiency certainly assists guidance counselors during their encounters with aggressive parents.

School Social Workers

As a school social worker, I am very aware of the importance of good parental relationships. Whereas guidance counselors often engage in more in-depth relationships with students, school social workers share similar in-depth relationships with the parents of these students. I reason that the healthier this relationship, the easier it becomes to assist the student. Conversely, volatility in the social worker/parent relationship complicates the process of providing assistance to a student. Turbulence for school social workers occurs when parents disagree with their decisions or recommendations.

Several factors make school social workers prone to parental aggression, including the nature of their involvement with the parent. These relationships are quite different from other parent/school personnel relationships. Social workers address a wide variety of student and family needs. Whether the problem is personal, community related, or school related, school social workers, together with parents, work to overcome a variety of issues. Periodically, parents become confrontational or aggressive when their methods of parenting may not be aligned with the best interests of their child. Any recommendations by the school social worker to this effect occasionally result in less-than-pleasant interactions with the parent.

At times, parents may perceive the school social worker as a savior of sorts, in that these professionals provide services or steer the parents toward resources that assuage many difficulties. When services are not delivered or accessible to the parent for any number of reasons, the social worker can become the focus of aggression or hostility.

Another concern for school social workers is the fact that they often meet at residences to discuss an issue or issues involving the student or his or her family. Although this gives the social worker a great opportunity to observe the student's home environment, it also unfortunately removes the social worker from the protection of the school campus. When acting as a liaison between the parent and the school, the school social worker must exercise the utmost caution if the parent becomes aggressive or hostile.

School Health Personnel

In what way could a parent become confrontational or aggressive toward school health personnel? A logical response would be, "Why would they?" School health personnel simply try to assist students with medical issues. Where could problems possibly arise?

I have heard health personnel discuss their experiences with parents and was surprised to discover that parents do indeed become angry or hostile for a number of reasons. After discussing these encounters, I concluded that school health personnel often function in one (or all) of three capacities. First, as medical care providers; second, as information suppliers; and third, as suggestion givers.

In their capacity as medical care providers, school health personnel dispense medication and tend to injuries or illnesses. Their encounters with parents remain, for the most part, free from turbulence because students have medical needs that are immediately met by these personnel. As information suppliers, school health personnel must often contact parents in an effort to relay information regarding the child's medical issue. Various problems such as required medication, injury, need for outside medical attention, poor hygiene, or lack of medical requirements (e.g., immunizations) are all issues that may aggravate parents and result in aggressive behavior toward health care personnel. Finally, as suggestion givers, health care personnel find themselves in the tenuous position of suggesting to the parents what would be most beneficial for their child. For example, a school nurse informs a parent that his or her child's medication may require adjustment because the child becomes drowsy in class. It is possible that the parent may take this simple suggestion as an affront because he or she perceives that the nurse is claiming to know what is best for the child. Taken a step further, that parent could also interpret the request as an indication that he or she is not an adequate parent. As a result of these misperceptions, parental hostility may emerge. Whether acting as a care provider, information supplier, or suggestion giver, health care professionals may draw the ire of parents. As inconceivable as it may seem, they, too, must exercise caution when interacting with parents.

OFFICE PERSONNEL

When a parent contacts a school, the first professionals with whom he or she usually communicates are office personnel. Whether a parent arrives on campus and enters the front office or communicates with the school via telephone, office personnel are usually the initial school contacts.

Office personnel, who serve in at minimum two capacities, also play a major role in the school's attempt to address the actions of aggressive or confrontational parents. First, as initial observers, they note the actions or behaviors of a parent from the moment the parent enters the school. At this point, they can gauge the parent's level of hostility and also observe if the angry parent is carrying a weapon, is inebriated, or is accompanied by another person. As the initial observers, office personnel are in the optimal position to assess the degree of difficulty that the parent may subsequently present. Second, office personnel serve as informers. If necessary, they must communicate to their colleagues the parent's arrival and disposition. This valuable information is relayed to other professionals, who then decide whether to meet with the parent.

For several reasons, office personnel find themselves at a disadvantage when encountering confrontational parents. First, there is usually little warning of a parent's arrival on campus. Consequently, they are unable to prepare for the encounter because they are often unaware of the issues that have resulted in the parent's aggressiveness. Second, office personnel are physically exposed to verbal or physical threats because they are usually positioned in the front of the school. This physical positioning differs from that of other types of personnel, who have the option to delay or cancel a meeting if concerned about an overly aggressive parent. Borrowing a military term, office personnel are on the front line, and this position occasionally lends itself to difficulties.

School Psychologists

School psychologists provide comprehensive, multifactored, multisourced evaluations; engage in counseling; and provide consultation among their duties. These professionals might also encounter parental aggression because they frequently meet with parents. One example of turbulence between school psychologists and parents might be a parent's reaction to his or her child's performance on an evaluation. In this capacity, school psychologists are cast in the role of information supplier, because they must interpret the results of the evaluation. As the school psychologist provides the results to the child's parent, these findings may not meet the realistic or unrealistic expectations that the parent has set for the child. If expectations are not met, the parent could consider the school psychologist the bearer of bad news and, consequently, react aggressively. The parent may also view the school psychologist as a judge of his or her child, although this, of course, could not be further from the truth. This perception may be even more prevalent if the child has performed poorly on the assessment. The identification of learning weaknesses, or disagreement with recommendations or options, could also conceivably result in aggressiveness.

While one father demands to know why his son is not "gifted," a mother may be irate that her daughter has been classified as "mentally handicapped." These are highly sensitive areas that, if not handled with extreme caution, could easily escalate to an intense interaction between the school psychologist and parent.

In addition to the aforementioned issues, school psychologists might report initial assessment findings and recommendations to the parents without colleagues present. This arrangement lends itself to possible problems, because any form of parental aggression is magnified without the presence of other school personnel. This situation is similar to the teacher who has a conference night meeting alone with a parent in his or her classroom, or a guidance counselor who invites a parent to discuss a volatile issue in his or her guidance office.

OTHER SCHOOL PERSONNEL

Other types of school personnel can come into contact with aggressive parents. For example, maintenance personnel, cafeteria workers, or crossing guards might encounter a confrontational parent in the course of their daily duties. Per the No Child Left Behind Act, home-school liaisons also have occasional interactions with parents, which can conceivably deteriorate into problematic situations for these important personnel.

QUESTIONS FOR DISCUSSION

1. Does your job description create a disadvantage for you regarding interactions with potentially aggressive parents? During these encounters, does your job description provide any advantages?

2. Have you ever witnessed a colleague in a heated encounter with a parent? Could this colleague have done anything differently to possibly lessen the intensity of the situation?

3. Do you have a prearranged plan or approach that could be implemented easily if you encountered an aggressive or hostile parent? If not, do you think a plan of this nature would be worthwhile?

PART II

Addressing Parental Aggression

CHAPTER FOUR

The RAID Approach

WHAT HAVE WE ESTABLISHED SO FAR?

We have established several key points, including the fact that parental aggression is a relatively obscure and unique problem that is considered a pertinent issue by many school professionals. We discovered what specific types of aggression parents exhibit toward school staff, and that aggressive acts can range in severity and have different effects on school personnel. From verbal threats to physical intimidation, no type of aggressive act is without effect on the school employee. Also, we know that parental aggression occurs more frequently than suspected, especially verbal acts of aggression. In addition, we established that parental aggression could be directed toward any type of school personnel.

Although specific types of personnel have more frequent contacts with parents (i.e., school administrators), other types of personnel also come in contact with parents on many occasions during the school year. Unfortunately, some of these interactions may result in volatile encounters with parents or guardians. Finally, we established that educators have traditionally maintained a reactive stance with regard to their dealings with aggressive parents.

With all of these facts taken into consideration, one critical question remains: "What can school personnel do to actually address the problem of parental aggression?" I concluded that an effective approach for working with aggressive parents would benefit school personnel greatly, and it was well past due.

Before I began to construct an approach to address the problem of parental aggression toward school personnel, I thought it would be prudent to explore existing approaches on this topic. I found copious amounts of literature available on approaches that addressed student hostility; however, much less existed in the area of school personnel and parent hostility. Most notably, the works of Blauvelt (2001), Margolis (1990; Margolis & Tewell, 1988), McEwan (1998), Storey (1990), and Whitaker and Fiore (2001) address parental aggression toward school personnel. These authors have also provided techniques and suggestions to be implemented during interactions with hostile parents or guardians.

Although the works of the aforementioned authors are invaluable, as I noted, little existed regarding *proactive* approaches to parental aggression toward school personnel. As a result, I decided to create an approach that specifically addressed the avoidance or reduction of turbulence before the actual meeting with the parent begins. I call this the RAID Approach.

SEVEN FREQUENTLY ASKED QUESTIONS REGARDING THE RAID APPROACH

The following seven questions have been the most frequently asked in regard to the RAID Approach:

1. What does RAID stand for?

RAID is an acronym for

> **R**ecognizing
>
> **A**ssessing
>
> **I**dentifying
>
> **D**iffusing

These four steps—recognizing the potential for a volatile encounter, assessing your ability to emotionally handle the situation, identifying your advantages, and diffusing the parent's anger during the initial approach and greeting—comprise the RAID Approach.

2. What is the ultimate goal of the RAID Approach?

The RAID Approach is intended to be a practical tool for school employees in their efforts to effectively interact with hostile or aggressive parents. The RAID Approach is not an "end to a mean" because this approach may not completely eradicate problems between school personnel and aggressive parents. The RAID Approach remains, however, a preemptive technique in which the main goal is the reduction of parental aggression. If parental aggression or hostility is reduced, or even eliminated, a more favorable chance of securing a solution to the problem may result. This outcome benefits the student, parent, and school employee, and, in addition, the school campus becomes a safer environment.

3. Where can the RAID Approach be applied? Who can apply it?

The RAID Approach can be applied at the elementary, middle, and secondary school levels. In addition, the approach can be implemented in special education settings or alternative schools. The RAID Approach is a realistic option in any school setting in which a parent interacts with school personnel. Any type of school personnel—from school superintendents to front-office workers— can use the RAID Approach effectively. It should be emphasized, however, that as noted earlier in this chapter, the effectiveness of the RAID Approach relies on its multidisciplinary approach to parental aggression. The involvement of various school personnel is essential in the majority of situations in which parents or guardians become aggressive.

4. What are the RAID Approach's main limitations?

There are several limitations to the RAID Approach. Most notable is that the approach does not address or reduce parental hostility after formal meetings or conferences have begun. This approach is meant as an option to be used *prior* to formal meetings, as school personnel initially engage aggressive parents. By attempting to gauge or reduce hostility prior to the meeting, it is intended that subsequent interactions between parents and school personnel will be less volatile as the formal meeting commences.

Another limitation of the RAID approach is its dependence on a variety of school personnel for effectiveness. This multidisciplinary approach requires a major commitment from all school personnel. It is the task of school administrators to ensure that all personnel consider the importance of this schoolwide approach.

The RAID Approach, for obvious reasons, also may not be effective with individuals who are mentally or emotionally unstable. In addition, the approach also benefits from the presence of an on-campus school resource officer. Unfortunately, these officers are not available at many schools.

5. Could the RAID Approach be used with individuals other than parents?

Definitely. The RAID Approach could be implemented to address hostility exhibited by several types of individuals. For example, hostile students or angry school personnel might also present problems similar to those of a parent. Caution and the need for a preemptive approach to their aggressiveness are, indeed, also warranted. The simplicity and practicality of the RAID Approach makes it flexible in a variety of other situations involving individuals other than parents. For the purposes of this book, however, the RAID Approach will focus solely on aggression or hostility perpetrated specifically by parents or guardians.

6. Does the RAID Approach contain hidden benefits?

I can identify three hidden benefits that may be gained as a result of the implementation of the RAID Approach. First, by effectively addressing parental aggression and hostility by means of this approach, school personnel and students are spared from witnessing explosive encounters between angry parents and school personnel. It is not unrealistic to expect that students should not have to observe adults exhibiting negative behaviors at school. Unfortunately, though, students, especially those who assist school personnel in front offices, often come into contact with angry parents who intend to direct their emotions toward adult school personnel. Although parents will rarely intentionally direct their aggression at students, the students may still be affected by these encounters.

Traditionally, schools tend to exercise formal procedures that target a wide variety of issues. These procedures exist in the hope of gaining a sense of control in specific situations and, ultimately, returning the school to its normal state of functioning. For example, many schools have crisis intervention plans or fire or tornado procedures. Civility policies are also established with the intent of addressing general behaviors on school campuses. A second benefit of the RAID Approach is that it also attempts to provide a sense of control over the behaviors of volatile parents. This sense of control is recognized and valued by many types of personnel as they attempt to perform their duties on their school campuses.

Finally, the RAID Approach may provide hidden benefits in two areas: staff cohesiveness and reduction of responsibility. An increase in staff cohesion could result because the RAID Approach's multidisciplinary nature lends itself to the involvement of various school personnel as they attempt to diffuse a potentially volatile encounter. This team approach to aggression can realistically serve to improve staff cohesiveness. In addition, if applied properly, the RAID Approach can reduce the amount of responsibility placed on any one individual. For instance, by executing its multidisciplinary approach, several professionals work to identify and help to diffuse parental aggression. As a result, the onus is not placed solely on one professional to alleviate the parent's anger, but on that professional and his or her colleagues.

7. What can sabotage the effective implementation of the RAID Approach?

Several actions can severely reduce the effectiveness of the RAID Approach, the first of which is possessing an "I can handle this myself" mind-set. This will, of course, sabotage the multidisciplinary nature of the RAID Approach.

Second, I suggest discussing how to use the RAID Approach. The RAID Approach is intended for year-round use. Therefore, the RAID Approach should be implemented at the beginning of the school year. To delay implementation increases the likelihood of unfavorable encounters between school personnel and parents.

Third, and possibly most damaging to the effectiveness or implementation of the RAID Approach, is the failure of school personnel to recognize the importance of parental aggression. This lack of acknowledgment could significantly reduce the commitment exhibited by school personnel in executing the approach. Throughout the nation, there has been heightened awareness regarding various forms of aggression within schools. Aggression perpetrated by parents and guardians should not be overlooked.

Before I identify the inner workings of the approach, let me explain some of its features. First, the approach is "commonsensical." Second, it is a schoolwide, multidisciplinary approach toward parental aggression. Third, the RAID Approach possesses two qualities: brevity and simplicity. These three features are imperative to the RAID Approach's overall effectiveness.

JUST COMMON SENSE

As in most other situations in our lives, common sense probably remains the most effective means of resolving a problem. Ironically, this simplest and most effective of tools remains frequently overlooked. Throughout my years of observing school personnel and their interactions with aggressive parents, I have become aware of the frequent absence of common sense during these circumstances. I've witnessed many types of school personnel not employing basic techniques that could have easily diffused these volatile situations. Why are these techniques ignored? I can speculate that either the professionals weren't aware of the technique or they considered the technique almost too simple to be effective. I think both reasons are acceptable, at least until professionals are made aware of other effective techniques and their subsequent value.

Commonsense techniques make the application of the RAID Approach much easier, and the avoidance of complicated techniques also reduces the likelihood that these techniques would be ignored by school personnel. Also, this commonsense approach makes its use appealing to many different types of school personnel. I can recall one discussion with a staffing compliance specialist regarding the RAID Approach. After I had finished my description of the approach, she noted, "These are simple techniques that I'm already aware of, I just don't use them because I don't think of them when I really need to." This feedback was exactly what I hoped to hear when I constructed the RAID Approach, because RAID relies heavily on the use of overlooked, but commonsense techniques.

A SCHOOLWIDE, MULTIDISCIPLINARY APPROACH TO PARENTAL AGGRESSION

I think it is natural for an employee to attempt to handle an aggressive parent alone. I also feel that there are several reasons for this tendency. First, professionals may have the misperception that colleagues would feel negatively toward them if they could not handle the parent effectively by themselves. This mind-set could lead to unnecessary and unavoidable encounters if additional personnel were involved. It is my opinion, however, that the main reason for an individual approach to parent aggression is the lack of an established multidisciplinary approach for school personnel. The establishment of the RAID Approach's multidisciplinary style guarantees that several individuals will maintain active roles in the remediation of the problem. This is a commitment that must be adopted if the approach is to be effective. If a schoolwide commitment to parental aggression is to be adopted, school principals and other administrative staff will have a major role in relating the importance of the issue and the necessary multidisciplinary approach to school personnel. If administrators expound the value of a multidisciplinary approach to parental aggression, other school personnel may be more willing to become involved in the process.

BREVITY AND SIMPLICITY

Most school personnel have been exposed to some type of method or approach that consists of numerous steps to address student behavioral or academic concerns. I have been known to frown upon "cookbook" approaches that consist of far too many steps for practical implementation. The main problem with these approaches is the necessity to have the cookbook in front of you at the time of the approach's implementation. Needless to say, this is not realistic or practical for personnel when encountering aggressive parents. A simple approach to aggressiveness is far more easily applied by school personnel, and the brevity of the RAID Approach ensures that it will be implemented more consistently, which might result in more effective intervention for school personnel.

In addition to the RAID Approach's brevity, I felt that the approach should be easy in its application. As I mentioned earlier in this chapter, simple, commonsense techniques stand a higher probability of being implemented effectively than do complicated techniques. These simple techniques are also more accessible to a wider variety of school personnel. For example, using the RAID Approach, a principal, office worker, or school social worker could access identical techniques. This simplicity is not just desirable, but necessary.

It is difficult to quantitatively assess the effectiveness of the RAID Approach; however, I have received a significant amount of feedback regarding the approach's techniques. Fortunately, school personnel feedback has been very favorable. Short but simple techniques greatly enhance the effectiveness of the RAID Approach.

I hope that the questions and the characteristics described earlier in this chapter provide an understandable framework for the RAID Approach. This simple but brief model was constructed with the intent of not placing the entire responsibility for dealing with hostile parents on one specific professional. The success of this approach— like any other school-related mission or activity—depends on the attitude and commitment of the school personnel who implement it. If implemented properly, the RAID Approach can lessen the burdensome task of interacting with hostile parents.

Now that the philosophy and generalities of the RAID Approach have been identified and discussed, it is necessary to provide an in-depth description of the approach's four steps. For purposes of review, the steps are

Recognizing the potential for a volatile encounter

Assessing your ability to handle the situation

Identifying your advantages

Diffusing the parent's anger during the initial approach and greeting

I will devote one chapter to each step of the RAID Approach. Scenarios and interviews that most accurately illustrate the obstacles involved in volatile parental encounters will also be provided. I usually alert potential RAID Approach users that many of the suggestions and techniques may seem to be very basic or commonsensical. Regardless, this feature is one of the main advantages of the RAID Approach. Most educational professionals maintain these techniques in their repertoires, but, unfortunately, they are often overlooked during volatile encounters. The next chapter will address Step One of the RAID Approach, "Recognizing the Potential for a Volatile Encounter."

QUESTIONS FOR DISCUSSION

1. Do you feel that common sense is overlooked during encounters with aggressive individuals? Can you recall a circumstance when you overlooked a commonsense option that might have helped deescalate a tense situation?

2. One of the features of the RAID Approach is its schoolwide team approach toward dealing with aggressive or confrontational individuals. Do you feel that your school or district would be receptive to this type of approach?

3. Traditionally, how has parental aggression been dealt with in your school? Do you consider your school's manner of addressing confrontational or aggressive parents effective?

CHAPTER FIVE

RAID Step One

Recognizing the Potential
for a Volatile Encounter

I believe that most professionals in the field of education have a strong desire to help others. We really don't think of educators as helpers in the traditional sense, but in reality, it is one of the things that they do best. I've never met a professional who flatly refused to provide assistance to a student or his or her family members. Along with this desire to help, I think that a great majority of school personnel sincerely want to communicate effectively with students and their families. If problems emerge, most staff members want to make the situation right for all involved. Although this quality is admirable, it can pose enormous difficulties for the personnel when they engage aggressive or hostile parents. Unfortunately, some school personnel have a tendency to move immediately to assuage any issue or problem that the parent may present, regardless of the parent's demeanor. This often places the professional in a truly dangerous position because he or she may be unprepared for the parent's aggressive behavior. Moving forward too quickly and without caution is an invitation to unnecessary problems.

The RAID Approach contains four distinct steps, but no step is more critical than Step One: Recognizing the Potential for a Volatile Encounter. Logically, if school employees had the ability to make this assessment correctly and consistently, it is likely they would rarely be involved in an unpleasant or dangerous encounter with a parent.

To Meet or Not to Meet

Step One is activated when a colleague informs a staff member that a potentially troublesome parent desires to meet with him or her. The parent's arrival is usually unexpected in this case, however, the parent may also communicate his or her intention to meet with the staff member via telephone, letter, or e-mail. After being made aware of the parent's arrival or intentions, the staff member should have the option to meet or not meet with the parent. This decision often depends on the staff member's level of comfort regarding the parent's or guardian's disposition (we will discuss the topic of choosing not to meet a parent later in this chapter).

I strongly recommend that under no circumstances should a parent be permitted to go directly to the location of the staff member if another professional has not yet had an opportunity to gauge the parent's level of hostility. It amazes me how schools continue to be incognizant of parents simply arriving at classrooms to discuss issues with teachers without first checking in at the front office. This recommendation is especially important if the parent has previously been hostile toward the staff member via e-mail, telephone, letter, or face-to-face communication. As a matter of procedure, I recommend that schools have someone "in between" the parent and the staff member with whom he or she has asked to meet. These colleagues act as an initial screener for the staff member. Optimal school personnel for this task are front-office workers, administrative staff, or any other personnel located in the front of the school where visitors report. The purposes of this arrangement are, first, to have these professionals initially assess the parent's level of volatility, and, second, to have them notify their colleague immediately if the parent's disposition or behavior could present a threat.

It is also imperative that the colleague who initially comes into contact with the parent (usually front-office personnel) actually walks to the staff member's location to inform him or her of the parent's arrival. At this time, the colleague can privately inform the staff member of the parent's demeanor or other important information without the parent's knowledge. The assessment of a potentially harmful situation should not be left to one staff member only. In other words, it might take several staff members to make this important initial assessment.

WHEN IS IT TOO RISKY TO MEET WITH A PARENT?

If a parent arrives unexpectedly on campus and a colleague (e.g., front-office worker) senses that he or she might be volatile but is not quite sure of the level of risk involved, the onus is now placed on the staff member with whom the parent requests a meeting. How does the staff member measure the chances of a turbulent encounter? In his or her mind, at what point does a parent cross the line in regard to his or her behaviors? It would be wonderful if a practical scale could be used to determine whether to proceed with a potentially aggressive parent, but, unfortunately, I'm not aware of one. Nonetheless, I can offer several considerations that may help staff members when making this important decision. For the purposes of illustration, I will discuss the issue of a sixth-grade teacher who must decide if a meeting with a parent presents undue risks.

Consider Previous Encounters

The first and most logical question for the teacher to consider is, Has she had previous encounters with the parent? If the two parties have indeed met, the teacher can recollect any behaviors or comments made by the parent that made her feel uncomfortable or unsafe. Was the parent cooperative? Was the parent socially appropriate? Was the parent rude and confrontational? These are easy questions to answer and can influence the teacher's decision to meet with the parent. What happens, however, if the teacher has not met the parent? What if a rumor existed that portrayed the parent in an unfavorable light? These are realistic concerns, but the situation could be ameliorated by information that could be gleaned from the teacher's colleagues.

Consider Information From Colleagues

When a teacher seeks information regarding a student's parents, he or she could simply contact the student's former teachers and gather as much information as possible.

Former teachers, guidance counselors, administrators, and so on can offer a wealth of valuable information on parental tendencies and behaviors (the choice to consult former school personnel could be made more difficult, of course, if the student attended a previous school and these school personnel are not readily available). The instructor is also working on a short time line, because the parent is waiting for the meeting to commence. The teacher should not, however, rush to meet the parent if some information is not acquired.

Consider Warnings

Don't neglect the seriousness of warnings made by the parent to any other school personnel. Even if the parent made these threats during a previous school year or toward other personnel (who may not even be currently employed at the school), threats are important indications that the parent may be aggressive in his or her usual method of communication. The teacher should not take the chance that the parent's communication skills have improved. The teachers should also take seriously any comments made by students (e.g., "My mother really doesn't like you!"). Although this statement may be inaccurate, the meeting with the parent should not occur without the teacher being aware of the mother's possible attitude toward her.

Don't Discount Gut Feelings

Sometimes, the most accurate assessment we have about a situation is our gut feeling. For example, this reaction is a valuable guide regarding what type of communication style we think might work best with a specific student. Instinct and intuition also play a large part in deciding whether to interact with a parent whom you strongly suspect to be problematic. While not devaluing the importance of the aforementioned considerations, a staff member's gut feeling is valuable and should not be disregarded.

How Do You Say No?

After due consideration, the teacher might decide that it is not in her best interests to meet with the parent. The issue of deciding not to meet a parent takes some thought. Actually telling the parent that the meeting must be delayed or cancelled can be more taxing, and understandably so. When deciding to avoid an encounter, the parent may be informed of the teacher's decision in one of two ways. First, the teacher can inform front-office personnel of the decision to not meet with the parent. Reasons can include nonavailability, prior commitment, and so on. Front-office staff then relay this information to the parent and say that the teacher will contact him or her in the near future. Second, the teacher can inform the parent in person, but only with other school personnel in close proximity. Both options offer the teacher protection in the case of parental aggression. I respect personnel who make this decision because they usually reason that another meeting can always be arranged with other protective options in place.

It is also imperative that after the staff member decides to not meet the parent, he or she should immediately make school administration aware of the decision. During this follow-up session with a school administrator, options (safeguards) can be put in place for future meetings with the parent.

The "Guilts"

Ironically, the teacher's judicious decision to cancel a meeting might result in feelings of irresponsibility, guilt, incompetence, or even cowardice. But why? Aren't the teacher's reasons for the cancellation justified? In addition, why should the teacher subject herself to the possibility of unnecessary abuse? Although I agree with both of these rhetorical questions, I'm also cognizant that professionals occasionally experience guilt feelings after deciding not to meet a parent, even when it is the prudent thing to do. These feelings could be the result of several factors.

The "It's My Job" Mentality

This rationalization may be the biggest single reason for an individual's refusal to cancel or avoid a meeting with a potentially aggressive parent. An overwhelming sense of responsibility can dangerously override the employee's choice to take protective measures. "I have to meet with the parent, because it's basically my job to do it." This mind-set is not uncommon; however, it can be dangerous because other options are available that, when implemented, make the interaction with the parent safer and more productive. It's important not to ignore these options because of a false sense of responsibility. Parent interactions will always remain a part of the job of school personnel, but in no way should anyone place themselves in harm's way.

The Guilt of Passing on the Parent

When an educator considers canceling or avoiding a meeting with an aggressive parent, another coworker may have to address the parent's immediate concerns. For instance, the unsatisfied parent may demand to see an administrator instead of the teacher. As a result, the teacher may ask herself, "Why am I passing the parent to another colleague?" or, "Why should my colleagues have to deal with my problem?" At this point, the teacher may decide to meet the parent in spite of the parent's disposition. Of course, this is a dangerous decision, but nonetheless, I can see how the teacher reaches it. Fortunately, guilty reactions may be altered if the teacher simply realizes that she will probably have to interact with the parent in the near future. The next occasion, however, might find the teacher better prepared to exercise options that take the parent's behavior into consideration (e.g., having an administrator in the room during the meeting). It is clearly not an issue of simply passing a problem to another colleague, but rather having colleagues assist coworkers with the parent.

Cowardice and Incompetence?

Few professionals have intentionally cancelled a meeting with a parent without wondering if they could have done something else to remedy the situation. It's a great time for second-guessing and, yes, even questioning personal competence and courage. After a cancellation, I've seen personnel openly question whether they should have taken the chance to meet with the parent, even in spite of the parent's demeanor. These employees also wonder if their skills are broad enough to handle these challenging situations effectively. I usually point out to these personnel that the parent may have been agitated when he or she arrived at the school, and little could have been done to change his or her demeanor. I also challenge them to ask themselves why they would take the unnecessary risk of meeting with an aggressive parent in the first place? I also inform the staff members that although they are skilled employees, they probably have had little training in the area of parental aggression. It usually becomes immediately apparent to staff members that competence is not actually the issue. Although the issues of competence and courage do occasionally arise after a decision is made to not meet a parent, in actuality, competence and courage rarely have anything to do with the decision.

STEP ONE IN MOTION

The following is a scenario in which the sixth-grade teacher, Mrs. Smith, implements Step One of the RAID Approach with the intent of recognizing a potentially volatile situation.

Approximately 45 minutes after dismissal, Mrs. Smith is prepared to leave her classroom for the day. She is then informed by a front-office worker, via intercom, that a parent has arrived at the school demanding to speak with her. Mrs. Smith asks the office worker the name of the parent. After recognizing that the parent is the father of her most troublesome student, Mrs. Smith is certain that the issue concerns a recent detention assigned to the student. Two minutes later, the front-office worker arrives at the classroom and informs Mrs. Smith that the father appears to be very perturbed. The colleague also advises Mrs. Smith to approach the father with caution (the front-office worker has served her role as the initial observer and informer).

Mrs. Smith is uncomfortable with the father's reported demeanor and contacts an assistant principal requesting additional information about the father. The administrator explains that the father has a long history of difficulty relating to school personnel. He is also known to abuse drugs (the teacher has attempted to glean information about the father before agreeing to a meeting). Mrs. Smith contacts a fellow teacher who is familiar with the student's family. The teacher warns Mrs. Smith not to meet the father unless in a highly supervised setting, in the presence of the school resource officer or administrators. Mrs. Smith, however, reasons that she has a responsibility to meet with the father, especially in light of his son's behavioral difficulties. Nonetheless, Mrs. Smith decides that, overall, it would not be in her best interests to meet with the father (the teacher heeds warnings from colleagues and resists her feelings of obligation).

Next, Mrs. Smith asks the front-office worker to inform the father that a meeting will not be possible due to scheduling conflicts, and that she would contact the father on the following school day (teacher uses colleague to relay message regarding the rescheduling). After the father exits the campus, Mrs. Smith immediately contacts the assistant principal (because the principal is not on campus) and informs him of the father's aggressive demeanor and her decision not to participate in the meeting with the parent. Both discuss future options for the next meeting (the teacher uses this opportunity to include the administrator, and they are both able to prepare for the subsequent meeting with the father).

STEP ONE SUMMARY

This situation involved a teacher who wisely recognized the potential for a volatile or even dangerous encounter with a parent and who postponed the meeting request made by the father. In this scenario, there would be no need to proceed with Step Two of the RAID Approach. What would happen, however, if the father was not as perturbed, but he still posed concerns? What if Mrs. Smith decided to meet with him? It's important to realize that even "slightly perturbed" people should be approached with caution. The escalation of anger and the deterioration of an even mildly tense situation are issues that require special abilities and increased awareness by school personnel. Next, Step Two of the RAID Approach will address the staff member's ability to emotionally handle an aggressive parent in an effective manner.

STEP ONE CHECKLIST

After being informed of the parent's arrival, did you

   ___ Gather information on the parent before meeting with him or her?

   ___ Heed warnings about previous behaviors?

   ___ Recognize an urge to nonetheless meet with the parent?

___ Consider postponing or rescheduling the meeting if necessary?

___ Inform an administrator of the situation and plan to discuss future options?

QUESTIONS FOR DISCUSSION

1. Have you ever rushed into a situation and found yourself in an unpleasant confrontation with an aggressive person? In your opinion, why is it difficult for some personnel to hesitate before proceeding headlong into a possible conflict?

2. Have you ever refused to interact with a person who requested to meet with you because of his or her poor disposition or hostile nature? After deciding not to meet with the individual, did you experience any feelings of guilt?

3. After deciding against a meeting, did you contact a school administrator and apprise him or her of the situation? Was he or she supportive regarding your decision?

CHAPTER SIX

RAID Step Two

Assessing Your Ability to
Emotionally Handle the Situation

As mentioned in Chapter 5, one of the most admirable qualities of most educators is their desire to lend immediate assistance as most any situation dictates. Rarely do school personnel ask "Why?" when the request can ultimately benefit a student or colleague. We discovered, however, that this tendency to rush in might be problematic as it relates to encounters with aggressive individuals. To be sure, recognizing the potential for a volatile situation is a critical step toward assuring that the interaction with the parent does not become destructive or dangerous.

Step Two of the RAID Approach will explore school personnel's capacity to emotionally handle a situation involving a confrontational or aggressive parent. Once this brief assessment has been completed, school personnel can proceed more effectively and safely with the interaction.

If I surveyed 20 staff members after they implemented Step One of the RAID Approach, I wouldn't be surprised if all 20 of them considered themselves emotionally capable of engaging an aggressive parent. Why would there be such unanimity? One reason is a lack of awareness regarding the direct effect of personal emotions or issues on interpersonal relations. "Of course I don't allow personal matters or my disposition to interfere with my professional relationships!" This is a common response, especially because dragging personal matters to work is considered unprofessional. Nonetheless, on some occasions, emotional issues certainly do affect our interpersonal relationships with colleagues, students, and even their parents. "Not me!" you say? I often ask school personnel how many times they've arrived at school irritated, angry, or even depressed, and, of course, most acknowledge that at one time or another they've carried emotional baggage to work.

There are many understandable reasons for these emotions; but they become part of the staff member's ability to interact with people. It's a difficult challenge to keep our negative emotions apart from the many routine interpersonal interactions that occur during a school day, let alone encounters with challenging individuals.

School personnel are, of course, no less professional for experiencing normal emotions; however, they should also be aware of their capacity to effectively interact with a parent while experiencing heightened emotions. A staff member's emotions can exacerbate potentially volatile situations. Whereas Step One allowed us to explore whether the situation (as dictated by the parent's demeanor) was safe enough to proceed with the parental encounter, Step Two will permit a staff member to personally examine whether he or she can emotionally handle situations that may, in fact, be volatile in nature.

What Types of Issues Affect Our Emotions and Disposition?

It's interesting how personal difficulties outside the workplace seem to dissipate or at least lessen as the workday evolves. It seems as though staff members actually "decompress" during the course of the day. The reason for this could simply be the result of sharing positive interactions with students or colleagues. In addition, the many tasks of a routine school day might also prevent the employee from dwelling on the problem. These positive occurrences could help to lessen stress. Conversely, what would happen if the staff member—before he or she had a chance to decompress—came into contact with another individual who was also experiencing heightened emotions? Two highly emotional individuals brought together regarding a sensitive issue equals a volatile situation.

One way for school personnel to prevent the inclusion of personal issues or negative emotions into parental interactions is to simply be aware of the origins of their emotions. Negative emotions emanate from countless sources; however, the majority of these emotions can be traced to the staff member's home environment, the staff member's work environment, or previous unpleasant interactions with a parent or his or her child.

Any environment can produce numerous issues that might affect a staff member's mood on any given school day. Arguments with spouses, problems with children, or even an inconsiderate driver can contribute to a quick change in disposition before arriving at work. Wouldn't it be great if, upon arriving at work, there was some way of making us aware of our moods? We could delay our social interactions until we at least attempted to deal with the issue. The problem with this hypothetical situation is that many of us would refuse to even believe we were in a bad mood in the first place!

Has a colleague ever asked, "Is there anything wrong today? You seem upset." Typically, the response to that question is, "I'm fine . . . really I am." Later in the day, however, the same staff member who said "I'm fine" might be short with a colleague or less than patient with a student. This is unfortunate, because the staff member is probably well aware of the reasons for his or her poor disposition, and many times, it has nothing to do with what has occurred in the workplace. Later in this chapter, I will offer an option that could help staff members increase awareness of their dispositions.

I also would like to briefly mention another area of concern for staff members. As a crisis interventionist, I have had the opportunity to work with literally thousands of students and staff who were actively grieving over the loss of a significant person in their lives. I inform these individuals that the length of the grieving process cannot be estimated. I've witnessed people recover from a loss in a remarkably short period of time and return to normal functioning within the school setting. Others, however, require a much longer period to return to normal.

School personnel should be aware that while they are grieving, they might, in fact, perceive their behavior to be normal, whereas in reality, their moods have been drastically altered. The effects of grief should not be overlooked because they could definitely influence interpersonal communications with other individuals who might also be dealing with sensitive issues. Without a doubt, issues outside the workplace play a major role in our dispositions and ability to communicate effectively with a wide variety of people during a school day.

Moods or dispositions are also affected by the workplace itself. Few staff members could deny that on at least one occasion a colleague has angered them. A principal might be perceived as overly demanding, a teacher might not be viewed as a team player, or a front-office worker might be considered too outspoken. Most staff members have, at one time or another, been irritated or angered by a colleague.

Fortunately, most of these situations are resolvable and not considered overly problematic; however, a genuine problem arises when irritated staff members encounter another individual during a sensitive or potentially volatile situation. For example, Mr. Martin, a school psychologist, is repeatedly questioned in a condescending manner by his guidance counselor regarding the status of an assessment. Mr. Martin, who has indeed prioritized the assessment, is somewhat insulted. He informs the counselor that the evaluation has been completed and that it simply needs to be typed. This brief spat does not result in further problems (other than hurt feelings). However, a problem could emerge 20 minutes later when, in a completely separate case, Mr. Martin meets with a parent to discuss the results of her son's evaluation. The aggressive parent demands to know why her son has not qualified for the program for the Specific Learning Disabled.

Mr. Martin might react differently to the parent as a result of his previous encounter with the guidance counselor. It's obvious that negative confrontations, even with colleagues, can affect our subsequent communications with parents, who may also be in a negative emotional state.

A third area that can influence a staff member's disposition is when he or she simply dislikes the parent. I don't think this possibility is overlooked; rather, it is not usually verbalized by school personnel. For example, could a teacher actually dislike a parent, based on comments toward the teacher by the student, such as, "You know what? My father thinks you are a horrible teacher." Could a school social worker dislike a parent based on the parent's poor treatment of his or her child? Would a principal be remiss in not completely trusting a parent who, on one occasion, directed profanity toward him or her? I think you could answer yes to all of these questions. Although it would be wonderful if all staff members were genuinely fond of everyone with whom they come in contact, the fact remains that some people are easier to like than others.

When asked to explain the reason why someone doesn't like another person, how many times have you heard the response, "I can't put my finger on it, but that person just rubs me the wrong way"? This assessment remains safe as long as no contact with that person is required. However, if a meeting or encounter with the unliked individual is inevitable, this assessment can become problematic. At this point, the staff member's awareness of his or her parental perceptions is critical. By maintaining a high level of awareness, school personnel can modify or postpone encounters if their negative perception interferes with their ability to interact effectively with a parent.

Issues at home, with colleagues, or with parents can influence a staff member's emotions, disposition, and interpersonal communications with parents. However, staff members usually must proceed with the encounters while experiencing these emotions. One critical question emerges: At what point does the staff member decide that proceeding with an interaction might become turbulent or even dangerous?

FACE NUMBER FOUR

A good friend of mine recently found himself battling a very rare form of cancer. During one of my visits to see him in the hospital, I noticed on the wall adjacent to his bed a chart composed of seven pie-shaped faces. The first face illustrated a happy, "have a nice day" expression, and the remaining faces regressed to the seventh expression, which illustrated pain. This chart was intended for patients to describe to hospital personnel the level of pain that they were experiencing. I recall that the fourth face, a worried, anxious expression, was the point where the patient's discomfort necessitated attention by a nurse or doctor. It was imperative for the patient not to wait until the seventh face to describe his or her pain, because this delay might result in a longer relief period.

My friend miraculously recovered, but I remembered that pain chart. I often wondered if school personnel could somehow also refer to a chart, if only in their minds, that might allow them to realize when their emotional baggage might contribute to a volatile situation.

Every staff member has a Face Number Four, or a point at which a decision to proceed or not proceed with a meeting should be made. Unfortunately, we tend to wade right past Face Number Four and find ourselves staring at Face Number Seven. That is where the problems can easily emerge. Ironically, like the patient who refuses to acknowledge or inform hospital personnel of his or her level of pain, a staff member's refusal to acknowledge or be aware of his or her emotional state might result in his or her inability to handle a volatile situation effectively.

Try to construct your own stopping point, or, more simply, a point where you postpone or decide not to meet with a parent because of your emotional state. This simple task is more complicated than it appears. If we adhere to our hospital pain chart model, the first three faces would probably find school personnel more than willing to encounter aggressive parents. Face Number Four, however, could involve a situation where buttons can be irrevocably pushed and a loss of composure begins. Little, if nothing, constructive usually emerges from these interactions.

Most school personnel would agree that possessing the patience of Job is a prerequisite for entering the field of education. Most of these professionals would also acknowledge that if already in a highly emotional state, they might react uncharacteristically if provoked. There are many reasons why different types of school personnel lose their composure. A front-office worker might refuse to be "talked down to"; an assistant principal may be irritated when a parent goes over his or her head to the principal; or a teacher, after several months of attempting to remediate a student's behavior, is repeatedly sabotaged by a parent's lack of consistency at home.

We have all heard stories of school personnel having their intelligence, competency, or even their manhood or womanhood questioned. All of these situations may temporarily interfere with the staff member's ability to interact professionally with a challenging parent. Earlier in this chapter, I discussed the value of school personnel knowing the point at which they could be susceptible to provocation because of their heightened emotional state. Simply knowing what pushes your buttons before they are pushed goes a long way toward averting a possible conflict.

EARLY-WARNING COLLEAGUES

One of the benefits of working on a school campus is that most personnel have at least one friend or colleague whom they see on a regular basis. After becoming acquainted with a colleague, we are familiar with his or her professional style and habits. Along with knowing our coworker's usual manner of operation, we also become aware of his or her personality. We come to know his or her likes and dislikes, and what makes him or her tick. We are aware of the type of person he or she enjoys interacting, and conversely, what type of people he or she dislikes.

Colleagues usually know when something is bothering us. How often have we been asked, "What's the matter today? You are not acting like your old self," or "Woke up on the wrong side of the bed today, huh?" Our fellow workers are great early-warning detectors, yet how often do school personnel become engaged in turbulent encounters when, prior to the conflict, their colleagues were well aware of their heightened emotional state? One suggestion is for a staff member to ask a colleague to immediately inform him or her if it becomes apparent that his or her mood may interfere with social interactions. The staff member might even perform the same service for his or her colleague. Of course, only coworkers with whom one shares a reasonable level of comfort would be included in this arrangement. This option guarantees that a staff member won't enter an interaction without at least being cognizant of his or her disposition.

There is one caveat to this option, however: People sometimes become sensitive when informed of their poor disposition. If a colleague is thoughtful enough to bring this issue to the staff member, he or she shouldn't be viewed as anything but a coworker who is genuinely attempting to help the staff member avoid an unnecessary confrontation because of his or her disposition.

"I'LL BE BACK"

When a staff member realizes that his or her emotions might interfere with constructive interpersonal interactions with a parent, he or she should consider postponing the meeting. Might this aggravate the parent? Maybe. Might this pose a rescheduling problem for the staff member? Maybe. The benefits of cancellation, however, far outweigh the possibility of a turbulent encounter. Besides, deciding to postpone a meeting until heightened emotions subside is only a temporary delay. The staff member is not refusing to meet with the parent in the future, unless, of course, the parent is considered a real threat.

STEP TWO SUMMARY

After completing Step One, if a staff member decides to meet with a potentially aggressive or confrontational parent, he or she must next decide if he or she is emotionally capable of participating in the meeting. School personnel may experience many emotions that render them incapable of effectively communicating with a parent. Personal issues—both in and out of the school setting—and the parent's perceptions play a major role in the staff member's ability to interact effectively. A keen awareness of these emotions and perceptions is necessary, however, if they are not to interfere with a staff member's ability to address the needs and demands of a challenging parent.

School personnel need to establish ahead of time a hypothetical stopping point, or a point at which it becomes unconstructive to engage a parent. Personnel arrive at these stopping points when heightened emotions make attempts toward constructive communication unrealistic. The causes for arrival at this stopping point can originate from within or outside of the school setting, but an awareness of these emotions is essential for school personnel. Interestingly, colleagues are often overlooked with regard to helping a staff member become aware of his or her disposition. Finally, if emotions or perceptions could interfere with a parental interaction, the staff member should postpone the meeting rather than proceed and risk unnecessary difficulties. If the decision to meet a potentially volatile parent is made, Step Three identifies several options that might be implemented easily during these interactions.

STEP TWO CHECKLIST

If the parent does not appear hostile, and if you are considering proceeding with the encounter, have you

___ Become aware of your emotional state and parental perceptions?

___ Established a stopping point?

___ Asked a colleague to make you aware of your disposition if it could interfere with the interaction?

___ Considered not meeting with the parent if emotions or perceptions might interfere with the proceedings?

QUESTIONS FOR DISCUSSION

1. Do you tend to tackle problems at work regardless of your emotional state? Has this inclination ever presented difficulties for you?

2. Have heightened emotions ever affected your social interactions at work? Has a colleague brought this to your attention? If so, what was your reaction to this observation?

3. What type of person pushes your buttons? Is there a specific situation or statement that can be especially aggravating? How do you usually handle these circumstances?

CHAPTER SEVEN

RAID Step Three

Identifying Your Advantages

In Step One, school personnel can assess the potential for a volatile encounter, and in Step Two, they can assess their capability of emotionally handling a turbulent situation. Next, Step Three allows the professional to identify any advantages that remain available to him or her prior to an actual meeting with the parent. I can't help but recollect how many conflicts or explosive meetings might have been avoided if staff members had simply made use of these advantages.

Planning for a parental encounter using every option available is a logical step. It is ridiculous to engage in these encounters without the identification and implementation of every available advantage in order to secure an edge. Common sense dictates that these advantages almost always improve the chance for a successful encounter. Of course, parents are not "the enemy," but, on occasion, they can be intimidating or even threatening, and they require special planning efforts. Fortunately, these efforts—which include identifying and implementing advantages—may lessen the chance of a problematic situation arising for school personnel.

ADVANTAGES: WHAT'S AVAILABLE?

"Get the advantage! Gain the edge!" These are easy phrases to say, but before securing the advantage—and subsequently the edge—you must know where they lie within the school setting. Ironically, most advantages are directly under the noses of school personnel, but in volatile situations, they are often overlooked in the heat of the moment. I can best describe school personnel advantages (implemented during potentially volatile parent encounters) by dividing them into two categories: workforce advantages and environmental advantages (Jaksec, 2003).

WORKFORCE ADVANTAGES

Workforce advantages are school personnel capable of assisting a colleague during an encounter with a parent. In this section, I identify these personnel and describe their roles during encounters between their colleagues and parents. These personnel are not ranked in order of importance—because most types of school personnel (depending on the situation) can provide valuable assistance during a volatile encounter—nor is this list exhaustive.

School Resource Officers

Nothing affects an aggressive individual more quickly than the presence of a uniformed law enforcement officer. On campuses, these personnel are often known as school resource officers (SROs). These professionals work wonders during turbulent situations and provide a real sense of security for school personnel. One problem, however, is that in most school districts, SROs are not available in every school. For instance, elementary schools often have no consistent need for law enforcement personnel; these personnel are needed more frequently in middle and secondary school settings. If a problematic situation arises in an elementary school or a school without an SRO, a police street unit or another school's resource officer could be contacted. For the purposes of this chapter, however, let's suppose that the school is fortunate enough to have an SRO on its campus.

The primary role of SROs is to maintain order within and around the school campus. As mentioned, their mere presence can help to maintain stability. During an encounter that could become hostile or overly problematic, SROs can make their presence felt in three ways.

First, and least dramatically, SROs can make their presence known before the meeting commences. Once informed of a problem by school personnel, the officer might choose to simply walk by the meeting area and make himself or herself visible to the parent. This subtle identification usually indicates to the parent that law enforcement is quickly available if necessary.

Second, the SRO might actually attend the meeting that the staff member has agreed to conduct with the parent(s). If the staff member is aware of a parent's aggressive demeanor prior to the meeting, he or she should always make the SRO aware of the meeting well in advance. However, if the SRO is not available to attend the meeting, staff members might reconsider the prudence of the meeting with the parent and cancel or postpone it if any threat is perceived. I was once asked how to explain to a parent why an SRO was necessary at their meeting, even though the staff member felt the request was warranted. My response was, "If the situation has dictated the presence of an SRO, the explanation to the parent should be brief but honest. Explain to the parent that the nature of the situation and the emotions that have been displayed make the presence of the SRO necessary." The SRO's presence is for the benefit of both the parents and the staff members. No further explanation to the parent is necessary because safety is the primary concern. If the parent does not accept the explanation and becomes aggravated or even hostile, then the meeting probably would not be productive anyway.

Third, and most dramatically, SROs can directly engage parents if their actions threaten or harm school personnel in any way before, during, or after the meeting. Fortunately, most SROs are adept at deescalating situations before they become overly problematic.

Thus, the role of the SRO varies in intensity from simply walking by a room to participating in a meeting to, most dramatically, confronting a parent exhibiting aggressive behaviors. As much as we hope that these situations never occur, most educators have heard of stories involving hostile people being removed from a school campus by SROs or other law enforcement officers. Those lucky enough to have an SRO on their campus should not hesitate to use him or her in situations involving aggressive or confrontational parents.

School Administrators

An invitation for an administrator to attend a meeting with an aggressive parent can be a great advantage for school personnel. During these meetings, administrators are valuable because parents often perceive their presence as a validation of the importance of their concern. Subsequently, the parent's aggression may decrease. It is ironic, however, that although school personnel are usually fully capable of adequately addressing the issue at hand, the parent is more satisfied when an administrator is present at the meeting. But some school personnel will not request an administrator's presence even at a potentially turbulent meeting because they believe that their request is an indication that they are unable to handle the situation alone. In addition, some staff members feel that the administrator's presence is an indication to the parent that the administrator is acting as an arbiter or judge, even possibly or eventually siding with the parent. Both of these views are understandable; however, the value of an administrator's presence during a volatile encounter cannot be denied. Optimally, if a staff member becomes aware of an aggressive parent and is uncomfortable with the impending encounter, few types of school personnel possess the authority to maintain stability and provide support as do school administrators.

School administrators are very cognizant of the issue of parent aggression. As I discussed in Chapter 1, my studies on parental aggression toward school administrators discovered that these personnel were frequently the targets of parental aggression, especially verbal threats and accusations. Therefore, they typicaly have valuable experience with aggressive individuals. Other school personnel are certainly capable of interacting with aggressive parents, but school administrators can provide a welcome advantage, and they can be easily accessed during turbulent situations.

Front-Office Workers

Front-office workers find themselves in an advantageous position to assist their colleagues. They are usually the point of contact for people who arrive on campus angry or upset. As a result, front-office staff can inform coworkers of any behaviors that are perceived as threatening.

It is imperative that front-office workers are informed by school administrators (preferably prior to the start of the school year) that part of their job responsibility includes notifying the administrators or other designated school personnel if an aggressive parent arrives on campus. I also recommend that when front-office personnel observe the arrival of an aggressive parent, they should go immediately to the location of a designated staff member (e.g., a school resource officer or school administrator). Telephone communications should be avoided, because when face to face with the school resource officer or administrator, front-office personnel can inform that person of the parent's arrival, his or her demeanor, or any other concerns that they may have. For example, the parent may be inebriated or concealing a weapon.

The option to notify designated personnel in a face-to-face manner greatly reduces the chances of the parent becoming further aggravated by hearing the office worker describe the parent's behaviors or sharing concerns with his or her colleagues. This option also ensures that the officer or administrator will be well warned, prior to his or her actual contact with the parent. If the parent is deemed too volatile to meet with the requested staff member, typically the teacher, the administrator, or officer might wisely postpone or reschedule the meeting until further options or safeguards are secured and the teacher is afforded more protection.

Most front-office workers have a plenty of experience involving hostile or confrontational people. These personnel must, however, guard against gaining a false sense of security. Engaging a parent alone could unfortunately evolve into a dangerous situation.

Administrative Secretaries

Administrative secretaries may not always be located in the front of the school, but rather in rooms adjacent to the school's administrators. Consequently, they may not be aware of the arrival of an aggressive parent. So how can an administrative secretary possibly be considered an advantage for a staff member during a tense parental encounter? It simply takes a little "role creativity."

One unique role that secretaries can assume is that of an "intervener." For example, at the beginning of the year's preplanning period, a middle school principal discusses with her secretary and administrator some options during meetings with potentially aggressive parents. They arrange that upon being made aware of a possible conflict arising with a parent, Mrs. Larcom, the principal's secretary, is to interrupt the meeting after 15 to 20 minutes. As she enters the room, Mrs. Larcom asks the principal (or assistant principal), "Your 3:00 appointment called. Do you want me to cancel it?" A negative response indicates that the situation is nonproblematic, and no action by the secretary is necessary. Conversely, an affirmative response (e.g., "Yes, please cancel the appointment") signals that Mrs. Larcom should immediately contact another administrator or the school resource officer for assistance with the parent.

Secretaries can also assist other colleagues with this tactic during their meetings with potentially volatile parents. For example, a teacher might request this arrangement with a secretary if she feels that a conference night meeting could become emotionally charged.

In addition to providing a valuable opportunity for school personnel to indicate potential problems, this premeditated intrusion by the secretary also helps to break the rhythm of a meeting if it has acquired a negative, unconstructive tone.

Another interesting option is to invite the secretary to attend a potentially turbulent meeting with the obvious intention of taking notes. In reality, the secretary is closely observing the proceedings. If the situation deteriorates, the secretary can excuse himself or herself from the meeting and inform support personnel. If nothing transpires during the meeting, at least the secretary accumulated valuable notes!

Other Colleagues

In addition to resource officers, administrators, office workers, and secretaries, other school personnel can also provide an advantage for their colleagues during volatile encounters, as shown in the following examples.

Example #1

First-year nurse Ms. Nalin has arranged a meeting with a mother to discuss her son's sensitive medical issues. Prior to the meeting, the nurse voices trepidation; through her predecessor, she has been made aware of the mother's surly disposition. Ms. Nalin asks the school social worker to attend the meeting because she is aware that the mother is actually fond of the social worker. As the meeting commences, the mother appears very pleased to see the social worker, who informs the mother that she works closely on many cases with Ms. Nalin. With this awareness, the mother is very receptive to the nurse's suggestions and remains cordial throughout the meeting.

Example #2

Second-grade teacher Ms. Cunningham has had a running battle with a student's parents regarding their child's disrespectful tone in class. The parents have consistently defended their child, reasoning that his attitude is simply the result of a 13-year-old brother who presents severe behavioral difficulties. On at least two occasions, the parents have forcefully told the teacher to mind her own business. Nonetheless, the parents have requested a special conference with Ms. Cunningham. As a result of past experiences with the parents, the teacher (who does not feel comfortable inviting school administrators to the meeting) asks a physical education teacher to also attend the meeting. This is convenient because the student is also presenting similar difficulties in PE class. The meeting is conducted, and Ms. Cunningham feels more secure with a colleague present. Fortunately, the parents (in the presence of two staff members) appear to be more willing to discuss the matter without resorting to bullying.

Example #3

School personnel have contacted a child protection hotline regarding neglect issues involving a fifth-grade student. The father of the child is somehow made aware of the school's involvement. He arrives on campus demanding to speak with the registrar with the intention of withdrawing his son from school. Unfortunately, the principal, who is on campus, cannot be located. As the front-office worker informs the registrar of the father's arrival, both staff members decide to ask a teacher (who is standing nearby) to stand in the vicinity of the registrar's office until support personnel can be contacted. Without delay, the front-office worker searches for the principal, and when she is located, the administrator quickly proceeds to the registrar's office accompanied by a school resource officer from an adjacent high school. The situation is soon resolved with little difficulty.

In all three of these examples, school personnel did not hesitate to use colleagues in an effort to avert the escalation of an already tense situation. It should be emphasized that the nurse, social worker, and registrar all made plans to involve colleagues *prior* to their actual contact with the parent.

ENVIRONMENTAL ADVANTAGES

Environmental advantages could be defined as the addition, subtraction, or manipulation of any physical object(s) that might decrease the chance of aggressive behavior being directed toward school personnel. Gaining an environmental edge can be almost amusingly practical and commonsensical. You'll be surprised at the familiar nature of these advantages; however, like workforce advantages, school personnel unintentionally overlook environmental advantages. What follows are several environmental advantages that might be considered in tense situations.

Location of the Venue (Meeting Place)

The real estate agent's mantra, "location, location, location," really applies to school personnel when they are choosing a venue in which to meet with a volatile parent. When engaging these parents, one of the best ways to ensure a degree of protection is to consider where the meeting will actually be conducted. Conversely, school personnel who don't consider the location of their meeting might be inviting problems. For example, a teacher who agrees to meet with a highly emotional parent in a secluded or isolated room might be at a disadvantage; likewise for the school social worker who schedules an interview with a parent at his or her residence, all the while being well aware of the parent's past hostilities toward school personnel.

When deciding on a location for a meeting, the venue should always be in the proximity of coworkers who are in a position to lend assistance if necessary. A simple rule of thumb: Never agree to meet with a parent away from a populated area, such as a room at the end of a deserted hall or an office at the other end of the school. If school personnel are aware of an upcoming appointment with a parent, they should reserve a room well in advance. This prearrangement avoids the elimination of this valuable option.

Room Characteristics

Once a room with a good location has been secured, there are several other considerations within that room that school personnel might want to consider in order to increase their protection. These considerations include the size of the room, seating arrangements, doors, windows, and drapes.

Room size is important, although at many schools, available meeting rooms are at a premium. If the choice of room size is an option, however, a large room should be considered. This choice eliminates the cramped, closed-in feeling that may be exacerbated by the close proximity of an aggressive individual. The room should also be big enough to accommodate additional support personnel if their attendance at the meeting is necessary.

Seating arrangements are vital to the safety of school personnel. Nothing scares a person more than the feeling of being trapped in a room by an angry individual. There should always be a quick exit route from any room; however, improper seating arrangements can drastically interfere with these exit routes. I always recommend that staff members take the seat next to the closest exit to be sure they can leave the meeting if necessary. This option does not have to be obvious to the parent. Prior to the meeting, simply place a notepad on a seat to reserve your spot. It's never advisable to take the seat across the desk or table at the farthest point from the door. I have had many administrators describe situations where their exits were blocked by parents who had become angered. This is a frightening situation, to say the least.

Doors, windows, and drapes are often overlooked as items that provide advantages, but all three can have a positive impact for school personnel in turbulent situations. Ideally, every meeting location should have two doors. If the angered individual blocks one exit, you can simply use the other. Unfortunately, many rooms have only one door. In this situation, it is imperative to remember what was discussed regarding seating arrangement. Take the seat by the door!

In rooms with windows, you should open the windows during discussions and meetings. They should remain open to permit other school personnel to detect any type of shouting, loud outbursts, or other inappropriate communication that might indicate that you need help.

During tense meetings, drapes or blinds should also be opened to allow other personnel to check on the proceedings. Visibility is critical during these situations, and unopened drapes and blinds certainly negate this advantage for school personnel.

Unique Devices and Considerations

Electronic devices appear to be gaining increasing acceptance with school personnel in their efforts to get help during turbulent situations. During my presentations throughout the country, personnel have reported that intercoms and buzzers placed under the desks for immediate contact with other support personnel greatly aid their efforts to remain secure during volatile encounters.

Pete Blauvelt (2001) discovered that, surprisingly, the use of a basic mirror can be a great way for a parent to unknowingly reduce his or her anger. Blauvelt explained that a mirror can be strategically placed on a wall behind the staff member's desk or seat. The staff member then asks the parent to be seated and excuses him- or herself for several minutes. While the staff member is absent, the angered individual observes his or her reflection in the mirror and notices his or her unflattering facial expressions. As a result of this observation, his or her anger usually decreases. This clever option is often used by school administrators in their offices, but any staff member who has a room or office could also implement it.

School personnel have also informed me of the importance of making another party incapable of using weapons found in their own offices or rooms. Any object that can be thrown or held as a weapon could be used to intimidate or injure. These objects should be removed from the meeting area prior to the meeting. Obviously, chairs and large objects are not realistic candidates for removal; however, staplers, paperweights, desktop awards, letter openers, or even nameplates are all potential weapons that should be removed temporarily.

The best time of day to conduct a meeting is uncertain. Some might consider early-morning appointments the best opportunity to meet with a confrontational or aggressive parent. In addition, an early meeting might prevent the escalation of anger that could build throughout the day and culminate at the time of the meeting. Another train of thought, however, is that a meeting conducted at the end of the school day enables the parent to have ample time to be cognizant of his or her anger. Both make sense to me; however, both options also leave room for debate.

Step Three Summary

School personnel should consider two types of advantages before they decide to meet with a parent who may be confrontational or aggressive. A workforce advantage could be loosely defined as any colleague who might lend valuable support or protection during a volatile situation. An environmental advantage can be defined as any physical object that can be manipulated in an effort to decrease the chance of an altercation or unpleasant interaction. Both types of advantages are valuable, but unfortunately, they are also frequently overlooked. Next, Step Four of the RAID Approach will help school personnel diffuse parental aggression during their initial contact with the parent.

STEP THREE CHECKLIST

After deciding to meet with a parent and identifying your advantages, did you

____ Pre-identify supportive colleagues to join the parent meeting if necessary?

( ) Administrator

( ) School resource officer

( ) Secretary

( ) Other staff (e.g., school social worker, school psychologist, nurse, teacher, etc.)

____ Know the physical makeup of the room in which you will meet the parent(s)?

( ) Room's location in proximity to other school personnel

( ) Visibility (i.e., drapes, doors, lights)

( ) Access to exits

( ) Absence of items that could be used as weapons

( ) Presence of electronic devices (e.g., intercoms, buzzers)

QUESTIONS FOR DISCUSSION

1. Have you ever met an aggressive or confrontational person and felt that this person possessed an edge? What gave him

or her this edge? Could this edge have been due to the possibility that you may have not explored every advantage available?

2. Can you identify any advantages available at your school that were not mentioned in this chapter?

3. After witnessing an encounter involving an aggressive parent, can you recall the number of school personnel that actually helped resolve the situation?

CHAPTER EIGHT

RAID Step Four

*Diffusing Anger During the
Initial Approach and Greeting*

After completing the first three steps of the RAID Approach, school personnel should have a good sense of the potential for a turbulent encounter. In addition, they now should be cognizant of their emotional ability to handle the parental interaction effectively. The staff member has also identified valuable advantages within the workplace that might provide an edge during parental encounters. Finally, Step Four of the RAID Approach will allow school personnel to assess and diffuse the parent's anger prior to the start of the scheduled or unscheduled meeting.

A large amount of literature exists regarding methods for interacting with angry individuals during meetings or conferences (Jaksec, 2003). The overall purpose of the RAID Approach, however, is the assessment and reduction of aggression prior to the actual commencement of the meeting.

Let me provide an example of the rationale behind Step Four's preemptive nature. If a balloon is steadily filled with air, it will, of course, eventually burst. This continual increase of air in the balloon can be likened to the escalation of a parent's anger during a meeting with school personnel. As we have seen, a parent's "balloon" bursts for numerous reasons.

The RAID Approach's fourth and final step allows school personnel to recognize when the parent's balloon is going to burst and then helps release air (anger) from the balloon (parent) before the meeting commences. Of course, the parent's anger may not be completely eradicated by the staff member; however, Step Four could help reduce the chance of a parent entering a meeting in a highly agitated state and bursting his or her balloon.

Upon entering a school campus, a parent should never be permitted to proceed directly to a classroom or office, and as we have discussed, school personnel should always be informed of a parent's arrival *before* the time of the actual meeting. When a staff member is informed of a parent's arrival—and he or she agrees to meet with a parent—the staff member must then physically approach the parent. When school personnel make their way to the parent's location, whether it is at the front office or at the entrance of the classroom, their physical approach to the parent can make a significant difference during their subsequent interaction. Far too many times, school personnel wait until the actual meeting to meet the parent and then attempt to calm or deescalate a parent's anger. At that point, it may be too late.

How complicated can it be to approach a parent, greet him or her, and then invite the parent to meet with you? Every day, thousands of school personnel are involved in this simple engagement with no difficulty. Problems might emerge, however, when a highly emotional parent arrives on campus. Subsequently, the staff member's physical approach to the parent is much more important, and simple, overlooked factors become more critical. The proper demonstration of these techniques can strengthen communication between the parent and staff member. As a result, more open, constructive communication occurs, and this improved communication acts as a conduit for the rapid resolution of the problem at hand. Let's examine several techniques that might be implemented by school personnel in an effort to demonstrate to parents that they are not adversaries, but sincere help providers.

OBSERVING THE PARENT

The first type of contact between parent and staff member is visual. Whether opening a door, turning a corner, or walking down a hallway, school personnel first must actually see the parent before verbal interactions are initiated. Good eye contact is considered an expression of warmth or genuineness. Traditionally, good eye contact has been accepted in our society as an admirable habit. This brief visual contact between staff member and parent also remains a great opportunity to assess the parent in several important ways, but, unfortunately, school personnel often do not capitalize on this opportunity. The period between eye contact and actual verbal communication with a parent might be only seconds in length. Subsequently, it's imperative that during this time, school personnel focus intensely on the parent, all the while noting possible indicators of aggression or hostility.

A logical question at this point might be, "When eye contact is made with the parent, what exactly do school personnel look for?" Actually, school personnel should look for several things, all possible indicators of the parent's disposition.

Body Posture and Facial Expressions

When the parent comes into view, school personnel should immediately observe his or her body posture. If the parent is seated, does he or she appear rigid or tense? Is he or she leaning forward? If the parent is standing, is he or she pacing? Is he or she standing at attention with arms crossed? Maybe his or her back is intentionally facing the staff member. All of these postures indicate that the parent may be perturbed or not happy with the situation.

Facial expressions can also tell us much about a person's mood. Frowns, glares, eye rolling, or intimidating stares are indications that the individual should be approached with caution. Also, some people display "poker faces," and their emotions are very difficult to gauge.

Behavior

In addition to physical indicators, a parent's behavior should also be observed as the staff member makes his or her approach. The parent's first statements are strong indicators of his or her disposition, and this disposition might subsequently dictate the manner in which school personnel deal with the parent. An obnoxious response to an attempted pleasantry might result in an urge to retaliate verbally, but this response would probably result in further deterioration of the situation. School personnel should be wary of threatening statements, vulgarity, accusations, or a loud voice. These verbalizations are helpful warnings for the staff member, because they indicate that a parent's disposition might interfere with the proceedings. In these situations, one should consider rescheduling.

Companions and Apparel

Whereas one angry or confrontational person is difficult enough for school personnel to handle, two or more individuals make the situation that much more problematic. As the staff member approaches the parent, it is advisable to look for the presence of a companion. These companions might be harmless and just accompanying the parent for support, or they might also intend to vent their emotions in regard to the situation. If the staff member feels outnumbered or intimidated by the parent, the companion, or both, it is prudent to request additional staff support or a postponement of the meeting.

Many incidences of violence have occurred in our nation's schools. Too often, when students bring weapons to school, they are not detected until it is too late. Therefore, when a staff member approaches a parent, his or her apparel should be observed, because clothing can easily conceal weapons. Although frisking a person is an unrealistic option, any feeling that the parent might possess a weapon necessitates immediate action. But what would be a prudent plan of action if a weapon was strongly suspected? A simple option might be that the staff member approaches the parent, greets him or her, and informs the parent that he or she will return momentarily. Then, the staff member should go to an administrator or law enforcement officer and report the suspicion. The staff member should delay his or her return to the parent's location until support arrives. This hesitation has two benefits. First, it might prevent the parent from becoming increasingly agitated, and second, it protects staff members from possibly being harmed by the parent.

APPROACHING THE PARENT

One afternoon, I was watching *The Wizard of Oz* with my children and saw the scene where the Cowardly Lion was called to speak to Oz. Trembling, the Lion approached Oz but became so consumed with fear that he abruptly turned, ran down the hallway, and dove through a window. Although I've never witnessed a staff member experience the Lion's level of trepidation, physically approaching an aggressive or confrontational individual can be intimidating for any type of school personnel. A walk can say a lot about a person. A confident gait is a valuable asset, especially when a person is afraid.

A staff member's walk might convey to the parent that he or she is sure of his or her professionalism and confidence. Conversely, a poor approach might indicate that the staff member is insecure and possibly intimidated by the impending encounter. It's important to note that a staff member doesn't have to be muscular or tall to give a confident appearance. Some of the most unsure, timid approaches I have ever witnessed have been made by large men. On the other hand, some of the most confident gaits I've ever observed have been made by females who weigh less than 100 pounds! In my opinion, size truly has nothing to do with the staff member's ability to display confidence as he or she approaches a parent.

If possible, avoid slouching while walking. Although it's not necessary to look like a drill sergeant, an upright, enthusiastic, relaxed gait exudes confidence. In addition, the pace of the staff member's walk should not be overlooked. Walk briskly to the parent, but avoid sprinting. This prevents the parent from feeling uncomfortable or defensive as he or she is rushed by a staff member. Also, as the staff member approaches the parent, he or she should avoid talking to other school personnel. This simple oversight might indicate to the parent that more pressing matters exist. Although this may, in fact, be true, it is not advisable to indicate this to an already irritated parent.

Up to this point, the staff member has said nothing to the parent. Rather, as he or she approached, he or she closely observed the parent's posture, behavior, facial expressions, the presence of companions, and his or her apparel. The staff member has also given an appearance of confidence via his or her sure manner of approach. Now that the parent and staff member are in close proximity to each other, a verbal and physical greeting must occur. It is during this initial greeting that much of the parent's anger can be gauged and diffused. As a result, a less turbulent atmosphere might be established for the impending meeting or conference.

GREETING THE PARENT

As we have seen, the time it takes for a staff member to approach and observe a parent is usually brief. Similarly, the initial greeting also occurs quickly but remains a critical task for the staff member. How many times have we had a bad encounter with a person and thought, "Maybe we just got off to a bad start" or "I could tell from the beginning that there was going to be a problem"? So often, the nature of an encounter is dictated by what is said and done at the beginning. Lasting impressions are formed during these initial seconds, and sub-sequently, the importance of our physical approach, our words, and the manner of their presentation should never be underestimated. We will now examine several techniques that might result in the parent becoming more receptive and amenable toward constructive interactions with school personnel.

Facial Expressions

When a parent eventually comes in close proximity to the staff member, he or she will probably have to look directly at the staff member. What does he or she see? A scowling staff member increases the chances that the encounter will have a shaky start at best, because the parent might feel compelled to scowl back. A staff member displaying a condescending grin might result in a parent feeling at a disadvantage, and a defensive posture might be established. A parent might be insulted if a staff member is smirking and perceive it as an indication that the staff member doesn't consider the problem at hand to be overly important. All of these facial expressions can only add to the parent's level of dissatisfaction and make the staff member's job more arduous.

Have you ever attempted to argue with someone who is smiling? It's frustrating because it is almost impossible to do. This amusing fact can help staff members when they encounter perturbed or angry parents. Staff members might consider approaching parents with a genuine smile. This could be difficult, however, especially if the staff member is aware that the parent is not fond of him or her. I caution against an overly exuberant smile because it might indicate to the parent that the situation doesn't warrant serious attention. A simple, sincere smile can sometimes disarm the most volatile individuals.

Physically Greeting the Parent

Most professionals extend a hand in an effort to greet another person. The response from this offering can tell you a great deal about the recipient's disposition or intentions. Have you ever had a person attempt to break your hand with a handshake? Doesn't it seem that these people are attempting to intimidate or make a statement? In addition, by overtly refusing to offer his or her hand, a parent may be sending a blatant message to the staff member that the interaction is not welcome. It is never advisable for a staff member to insist on a handshake if the parent doesn't want to reciprocate, because this insistence might aggravate the parent. Genuinely offering their hand is a safe way for staff members to indicate to the parent that they welcome his or her presence and subsequent interaction.

I've observed staff members place their hands on a parent's shoulders in an effort to display genuine concern; this is a very nice but unwise gesture, especially with individuals with whom the staff member has little familiarity. My advice for school personnel: Play it safe. Simply offer a hand, and avoid any other form of contact with the parent. Many individuals might consider physical contact an actual sign of care or concern, but others might consider this contact an invasion of personal space and react erratically.

Verbally Greeting the Parent

The verbal greeting is the final task for staff members before they actually engage a parent in a formal meeting or conference. This greeting serves two purposes. First, it gives school personnel an opportunity to display their concern for the situation, and second, it allows school personnel to gauge the parent's level of anger.

"Hello" is, of course, the first word spoken by school personnel when they engage a parent. The words that follow "hello" are also very critical. People love to be acknowledged, even angry people. I recommend that after saying "hello" or "welcome," school personnel should always include the parent's last name. In addition, they should thank the parent for taking the time to come to school. For example, "Hello, Mrs. Smith. Thanks so much for coming in" or "Hello, Mr. Miller. Thank you for stopping by. I'm glad to see you." It may have been Mrs. Smith's or Mr. Miller's decision to come to the school, but thanks for their presence should always be voiced. These statements allow the parent to recognize the staff member as someone who appreciates his or her efforts and sincerely desires to resolve the problem. Overlooking this simple task might send a message that the parent isn't important, or worse, that he or she is like every other person who must be dealt with during the school day. Every person wants to feel special, including parents who want to believe that problems or issues are foremost in the staff member's mind.

The response to a staff member's greeting can be a great barometer of the parent's temperament. For example, a teacher might approach a father and say, "Hello, Mr. Thompson, thanks for coming in to talk." The father replies, "I'm not here for pleasantries. We have business to discuss!" This response is an early signal that the father may be aggressive or confrontational. As a result, steps might be taken to address his demeanor (e.g., invite another colleague to the meeting or have support staff in the vicinity). This response is in contrast to a mother who replies to the teacher, "No, thank *you!* I know you teachers are really busy." It is important to realize that the demeanor detected during the greeting is probably going to be evident in the meeting that follows.

SETTING PARAMETERS

Although the RAID Approach acts as a preventive screen for aggressive parents, some individuals may not exhibit aggressiveness until moments before the meeting, or after the meeting begins. Therefore, it is imperative to attempt to gauge the parent's level of anger via any of his or her verbalizations prior to the start of the meeting. Comments such as, "There's going to be big trouble here!" or "Somebody is implying that I am a liar!" should not be tolerated. If comments such as these are made, school personnel should inform the parent that in light of his or her comments, the meeting might not be possible. For example, after a mother has made mildly threatening statements, a nurse might inform her, "Mrs. Taylor, if you continue to talk in that manner, we will not be able to meet." If the parent gives any indication that his or her behavior will not cease, the meeting should be cancelled immediately.

After the staff member has greeted the parent and is confident that his or her response does not indicate further difficulties, an invitation to meet with the parent is made. The staff member should make this invitation, even if the parent is the one who requested the meeting. This is an opportunity to show the parent that the staff member is eager to help resolve the issue. The invitation should be simple but direct (e.g., "Mr. Jackson, do you mind if we meet in this room and discuss Jeffrey's math grade?"). This simple invitation gives the parent an opportunity to feel that he or she is in a position to effect change for his or her child. Also, it allows a response and offers the staff member another glimpse of the parent's communication style or demeanor. This is valuable information for the staff member who, during this time, is sizing up the parent and deciding if the meeting is in his or her best interests.

Once a parent and staff member actually sit down for the meeting, I recommend that school personnel once again thank the parent for coming to school. This reinforces the parental perception that the staff member is sincere in his or her intentions to resolve the issue.

STEP FOUR SUMMARY

Step Four is accomplished through two main tasks. First, the staff member must physically approach the parent, which allows him or her to observe specific indicators of anger such as body posture, facial expressions, behaviors, the presence of companions, and apparel. A gait can also be a valuable tool because it enables the staff member to exhibit confidence as he or she approaches a person who may be intimidating or angry. Second, the staff member must physically and verbally greet the parent.

The tasks of Step Four provide opportunities for school personnel to gain significant information regarding a parent's behavior and disposition. In addition, the parent may now view the staff member as someone willing to assist with the resolution of the problem instead of as an adversary.

It has likely become obvious that the RAID Approach addresses issues that occur prior to the actual meeting with the parent. As a result of these steps, parental aggression or confrontational demeanors might not be as prominent.

STEP FOUR CHECKLIST

When approaching a potentially aggressive parent, are you aware of your

_____ Eye contact?

_____ Body posture?

_____ Facial expression?

_____ Verbal greeting?

Are you aware of the parent's

___ Behaviors?

___ Posture?

___ Receptivity (e.g., handshake, eye contact, overall reaction to your greeting)?

Are you prepared to

___ Reschedule or terminate the appointment if the parent's behavior necessitates it?

___ Notify an administrator of any difficulties encountered?

QUESTIONS FOR DISCUSSION

1. Do you usually take the time to assess a parent's disposition prior to the actual meeting with him or her? Do you find this option valuable? If not, why not?

2. Which task in Step Four do you find most difficult? Approaching the parent? Verbally greeting the parent? Inviting the parent to discuss the issue or problem? Why do you consider that specific task difficult?

3. After approaching and greeting a parent, have you ever decided not to meet with him or her because he or she gave some indication that problems could occur?

CHAPTER NINE

Putting the RAID Approach to Work

The previous four chapters provided an in-depth look at the steps that form the RAID Approach. As we have seen, this approach is not overly complicated, but does insist that its users heed warnings and execute commonsense techniques. Unfortunately, school personnel overlook many of these techniques during their attempts to engage aggressive or hostile parents. To describe how the RAID Approach works, I will present a hypothetical scenario that involves a teacher and her encounter with two unhappy parents.

CASE #1: MRS. WINSLOW

Mrs. Winslow is a third-grade teacher in her second year of service. As part of preplanning activities prior to the start of the school year, she participated in a RAID Approach workshop. Mrs. Winslow recently divorced and is currently involved in a complicated and bitter child custody case. In November of the school year, she is contacted via letter that the parents of one of her students request a conference to discuss his behavioral performance. The student, Mark Morris, has severe behavioral problems and requires an inordinate amount of attention from the teacher. Past attempts to reach the Morrises have been unsuccessful, and Mark has recently been sent to the principal's office because of his behavior.

Mrs. Winslow telephones the Morris residence and introduces herself. A long uncomfortable pause follows. Finally, Mrs. Morris, in an irritated tone, says, "It's about time you finally got back to me, it's been two days!" Mrs. Winslow, somewhat stunned by this response, asks the mother if she and her husband would like to schedule a conference to discuss concerns regarding their son. Mrs. Morris responds affirmatively, but, in a barely audible tone, utters, "If he is sober, my husband might come, too."

As the day of the conference approaches, Mrs. Winslow informs school administrators of her concerns and possible options. The administrators are familiar with Mrs. Morris and indicate that although she is not overly involved in school functions, she hasn't presented problems for school personnel. Later, the school guidance counselor explains to Mrs. Winslow that the mother has recently married Mr. Morris, who, on two occasions, has become confrontational with school personnel when picking up his stepson after school.

Mrs. Winslow is in court on the day prior to the conference with the Morrises. On the day of the conference, she arrives at school emotionally upset because of the previous day's court appearance. She is also slightly nauseous. A fellow teacher, who has tea with Mrs. Winslow prior to the start of every school day, asks her if she is feeling well. The two teachers converse for 15 minutes. Afterwards, Mrs. Winslow decides that if she is not feeling better by lunch, it might be wise to reschedule the meeting with the Morrises. The day proceeds smoothly, and although emotionally fatigued, Mrs. Winslow, fully aware of her emotional state, decides that she is capable of meeting with the Morrises.

At 3:00, a front-office worker walks to Mrs. Winslow's room and informs her that the Morrises have arrived. She notes that the stepfather appears "woozy" and the mother seems agitated. Mrs. Winslow, although not feeling in charge of the situation, attempts to walk self-assuredly. As she turns the corner to approach the parents, Mrs. Winslow notices that Mr. Morris is standing tensely and Mrs. Morris is sitting with her arms tightly crossed. Both parents notice the teacher approaching and immediately look in the other direction. Mrs. Winslow approaches the mother, extends her hand, and says, "Hello, Mr. and Mrs. Morris, thank you for coming in today." Both parents barely respond to the greeting; however, the mother manages a slight smile and appears relieved to have finally met the teacher.

As they walk to the conference room, which is located in the main office area, Mrs. Winslow informs the parents that the principal will also be attending the meeting. Mrs. Morris seems at ease with this news, and proceeds to make a comment regarding the school's "positive atmosphere." As the parents follow Mrs. Winslow to the room, they are met by the principal, who introduces himself. Abruptly, Mr. Morris asks, "Now I understand. He's here because you can't handle the problem yourself!" Mrs. Winslow, firmly but professionally, informs the father that any more statements to that effect might jeopardize the meeting. The principal concurs, and, temporarily, the stepfather becomes more subdued. Mrs. Morris is embarrassed by her husband's remarks.

Mrs. Winslow and the principal have reserved seats in close proximity to the only doorway by placing their writing tablets on their chair seats prior to the start of the meeting. The seats are across the conference room table from the Morrises, not at each end of the table, which would be far enough away to create the illusion of "us versus them." The conference room drapes are drawn back, and, as the meeting commences, the door remains slightly ajar.

Mrs. Winslow describes Mark's performance, and, in an effort to remediate his poor behaviors, she recommends, among other options, improved teacher-parent communication. The father becomes increasingly agitated, and during the next 5 minutes, his behavior deteriorates dramatically and constructive communication becomes impossible. The principal's secretary (who has observed the father's behavior) interrupts the meeting and asks the principal, "Should I cancel your 4:30 appointment?" The principal replies, "Yes, cancel it." As the meeting resumes, the father abruptly stands up, shoves papers toward Mrs. Winslow, and directs an obscenity-filled statement toward the principal, chastising him for hiring "an incompetent fool." Fortunately, within minutes, a neighboring school's resource officer arrives at the room and escorts Mr. Morris off campus. Mrs. Morris is apologetic. After the mother leaves, Mrs. Winslow, the principal, and the guidance counselor meet and discuss the events that transpired. The teacher describes her feelings regarding the volatility of the father and overall tone of the meeting.

I've heard of many situations that are eerily similar to the incident involving Mrs. Winslow and her principal. Fortunately, this incident didn't result in harm to either staff member, but it easily could have. Was Mrs. Winslow lucky regarding the way this situation unfolded? Probably, but if we look closely, Mrs. Winslow also benefited from effectively implementing the RAID Approach. To clearly illustrate her use of the approach, let's dissect the decisions and options that helped her to avoid a very dangerous situation. For the purpose of review, the four steps of the RAID Approach consist of

Recognizing the potential for a volatile encounter

Assessing your ability to emotionally handle the situation

Identifying your advantages

Diffusing anger during initial approach and greeting

Step One: Recognizing the Potential for a Volatile Encounter

Mrs. Winslow was very observant regarding indications that the Morrises could be aggressive or confrontational. The first indication was detected after she made telephone contact with Mrs. Morris and heard these two comments: "It's about time you got back to me. It's been two days," and, "If my husband is sober, he might come too." Both statements increased Mrs. Winslow's concern regarding the parent's potential for confrontation. Based on this concern, she began to gather information from school administrators and the school guidance counselor regarding the Morrises' previous experiences with school personnel. Mrs. Winslow decided that, based on this information, the parents did not pose a threat, but precautions were necessary. Mrs. Winslow followed these procedures in Step One of the RAID Approach:

1. She gathered information regarding Mr. and Mrs. Morris.

2. She heeded warnings about Mr. Morris.

3. She informed an administrator and discussed her options.

Step Two: Assessing Your Ability to Emotionally Handle the Situation

Mrs. Winslow was experiencing significant stress because of personal issues resulting from a messy child custody case. Unfortunately, this situation appeared to affect her emotional state at school. In addition, Mrs. Winslow was aware of the perceptions that she had formed of the Morrises as a result of her previous telephone contact with the mother and information gathered from school personnel.

To ensure that her emotions would not interfere with her meeting with the Morrises, Mrs. Winslow established a stopping point when she decided to reschedule the meeting if she was not feeling better by lunchtime. This was done after a colleague mentioned to Mrs. Winslow that her poor mood was evident when she arrived at work.

Mrs. Winslow decided to proceed with the meeting after she functioned well during the school day. Finally, she considered herself emotionally capable of interacting with the Morrises and proceeded with the meeting. To summarize, Mrs. Winslow followed these procedures in Step Two.

She became acutely aware of her heightened emotions and perceptions of the Morrises.

She established a stopping point.

A colleague informed her of her disposition.

She decided that her emotions would not interfere with her ability to interact with the parents.

Step Three: Identifying Your Advantages

Mrs. Winslow activated workforce advantages in an effort to interact effectively with the Morrises. The teacher's workforce advantages consisted of efforts by the following colleagues, as described in the following section.

Administrator

After becoming aware of Mrs. Morris's attitude during their telephone conversation, Mrs. Winslow contacted a school administrator to inquire about the parent's previous interactions with school personnel.

Her principal was also present at the meeting with the Morrises and signaled to his secretary via code that support should be secured in light of the father's behavior.

Guidance Counselor

The guidance counselor lent valuable information regarding Mr. Morris's previous behaviors while picking up his stepson at school. The counselor also participated in the debriefing that followed the meeting with the Morrises.

Teacher

A fellow teacher brought Mrs. Winslow's disposition to her attention. She also acted as a signal to Mrs. Winslow that her mood could possibly interfere with her ability to interact effectively with the Morrises.

The teacher also allowed Mrs. Winslow to vent her emotions during their regular "tea session." This brief respite may have helped Mrs. Winslow function more adequately during the day.

Front Office Personnel

This colleague initially observed the arrival of the Morrises and then personally informed Mrs. Winslow of their arrival. The front-office worker also described the parents' disposition and other concerns to Mrs. Winslow, who used this input to prepare for her approach to the Morrises.

Administrative Secretary

Initially, the secretary walked past the conference room and observed the proceedings between the principal, teacher, and parents. The secretary interrupted the meeting when it became obvious that the tone of the meeting was negative and asked the principal if his 4:30 appointment needed to be cancelled. The administrator's affirmative response indicated that support personnel were necessary.

School Resource Officer

Fortunately, the resource officer arrived in time to remove Mr. Morris from the school for his volatile behavior. The officer was contacted by the administrative secretary after she interrupted the meeting and asked the principal the status of his "4:30 meeting."

The officer also may have informed the father of the ramifications of further aggression on a school campus.

Mrs. Winslow obviously benefited from the assistance of several colleagues, who composed workforce advantages, and she also intentionally implemented environmental advantages during her encounter with the Morrises. Some of Mrs. Winslow's environmental advantages included the following, listed on the next page.

Choice of Venue

Mrs. Winslow reserved the conference room for the meeting. Attempting to secure a venue after the parents arrived might have meant a location that isolated her and the principal from other school personnel. The room was located in a highly populated area adjacent to the main office. This afforded Mrs. Winslow the advantage of having school personnel in the vicinity if additional support was immediately necessary.

Visibility and Sound

The conference room drapes were opened prior to the meeting, because opening the drapes as the meeting commenced may have appeared obvious to the parents. The principal's secretary also decided to interrupt when the father's aggressive behavior became visible through the conference room window. The door remained slightly ajar, which allowed any type of loud verbalizations to be audible to school personnel outside the room.

Seating

Mrs. Winslow reserved the seats closest to the door in case an immediate exit was necessary for her and the assistant principal. It's also important to note that a large space between the parents and staff members may have resulted in the parents feeling intentionally isolated; subsequently, communication may have suffered.

To her benefit, Mrs. Winslow wisely employed workforce and environmental advantages during her encounter with the Morrises. Every advantage was activated prior to the arrival of the parents. These same advantages may have been significantly more difficult to implement after the meeting commenced.

Step Four: Diffusing Anger
During the Initial Approach and Greeting

Mrs. Winslow approached the Morrises carefully and began observing the couple immediately. As she confidently approached the Morrises, Mrs. Winslow noticed the tense posture of the stepfather. She also noted Mrs. Morris's crossed arms. The parents refused to make eye contact with Mrs. Winslow, whose handshake offering produced little feedback. These indications warned her of the possibility of an uncomfortable situation.

Mrs. Winslow thanked the parents for taking the time to come to the school and then informed the Morrises that the assistant principal would also attend the meeting. She correctly assessed that Mr. Morris's inappropriate response to the news of the assistant principal's invitation was an indication of potential difficulties. As she heard the stepfather's response, Mrs. Winslow firmly established that certain behaviors would not be tolerated as she informed him of the consequences of further inappropriate comments.

Mrs. Winslow also noted that Mrs. Morris appeared to be more eager for the meeting since their initial introduction.

Mrs. Winslow's approach and greeting served several purposes. First, the approach allowed her to observe and assess the physical characteristics and behaviors of both parents. Second, her verbal greeting appeared to have a calming effect on Mrs. Morris. Third, she informed the parents of the principal's invitation to the meeting. Fourth, after the stepfather's inappropriate remark, Mrs. Winslow established a parameter that prohibited these remarks from continuing. The teacher conducted all of these important actions in a very short period of time.

CASE #2: MRS. CANANSKI

Mr. Brown is a sixth-year middle school principal. His two assistant principals are unavailable for duty on this school day because one administrator is ill and the other is attending a mandated training. On the previous school day, Mr. Brown was informed that he was not chosen for a supervisory position within his school district. He was bitterly disappointed.

Early in the school day, Mr. Brown's secretary arrives at his office door and informs him that Mrs. Cananski, the parent of a recently enrolled student, is in the front office and wishes to speak with him. The parent, according to the secretary, appears agitated but not disruptive. The principal agrees to meet with Mrs. Cananski, but not before asking his secretary, school registrar, and guidance counselor to provide input regarding their dealings with the mother.

The secretary reports that she briefly observed Mrs. Cananski while she was enrolling her daughter the prior week. The guidance counselor says that she met the daughter regarding her schedule.

She notes that the daughter experienced behavioral difficulties at her previous school. The school registrar reports to the principal that Mrs. Cananski was "somewhat pushy" and "almost flippant" in the process of enrolling her daughter.

As Mr. Brown walks to the front office to meet Mrs. Cananski, he notices that she is looking out a window with her back toward him. The principal approaches her and says, "Hello, Mrs. Cananski, I'm glad you came in." He notices that the parent hesitates to turn around, and when she does, her facial expression indicates disgust. Mrs. Cananski weakly shakes the principal's hand and remains silent. An invitation is made to meet in his office, and the mother intentionally follows the principal at a distance.

As Mr. Brown invites Mrs. Cananski to have a seat, she immediately blurts out, "You have a real problem at this school." The principal calmly asks the mother to clarify her statement, and she says, "Kids are having sex in your school." The principal, somewhat shocked, asks, "Mrs. Cananski, where did you hear this?" She quickly responds, "My daughter." Mr. Brown suppresses the urge to chuckle and asks, "Mrs. Cananski, didn't your daughter just enroll at our school one week ago?" The mother responds, "It doesn't matter when she enrolled. The fact is, you are not running a good school, and you better do something about it quick."

As Mr. Brown becomes somewhat agitated at the mother's statements, he explains to Mrs. Cananski that personnel at his school have never been aware of students engaging in sexual activities. The mother arrogantly replies, "Well, you're having them now!" The principal, now becoming increasingly frustrated with the mother's refusal to accept his explanation, states, "Mrs. Cananski, as the principal, don't you think I would have been made aware of these activities if they were actually happening?" The mother responds, "Who knows? It's apparent that you have no idea what is going on in your own school." The principal now realizes that the discussion is going nowhere. His patience with Mrs. Cananski is wearing thin, although he realizes this may be due in part to his failure to secure a supervisory position.

The principal informs the mother that he will "look into the issue" and get back to her. Mrs. Cananski states, "I'm not done talking about this yet!" Mr. Brown stands and thanks her for coming in to meet with him. He then informs Mrs. Cananski that the meeting is indeed concluded, because he must attend to other administrative duties. The mother exits the principal's office immediately, but, while exiting the school, sarcastically announces to front-office personnel, "Great school you have here!"

Step One: Recognizing the Potential for a Volatile Encounter

The principal asks the secretary, guidance counselor, and school registrar about Mrs. Cananski's previous behaviors. He notes that the registrar had a poor impression of her. He also remembers that the guidance counselor explained that Mrs. Cananski's daughter experienced behavioral difficulties at her previous school, and one of the infractions was for kissing another student. With this information in hand, Mr. Brown decides that the potential for a volatile encounter is minimal and then proceeds to the second step of the RAID Approach.

Step Two: Assessing Your Ability to Emotionally Handle the Situation

Mr. Brown has always considered patience his strong suit. However, he is aware that limited patience (because of his failure to secure the district-level supervisor's position) could be a detriment during his meeting with Mrs. Cananski. With this in mind, the principal agreed to meet with the parent, but he also resolved to be aware of a possible increase of his level of frustration or agitation during the meeting with the parent. When his levels of tolerance became apparent to Mr. Brown, he decided to terminate the meeting. He also did not give in to Mrs. Cananski's desire to continue the meeting.

Mr. Brown was wise to realize that his emotional state could influence his ability to deal with Mrs. Cananski. On most occasions, Mr. Brown could easily address the unfounded complaints of the most persistent parent, but on this day, he was cognizant of his inability to interact with a demanding, somewhat irrational parent.

Summary

Interestingly, if we reexamine these situations, we see that school personnel can apply many of these options during their interactions with aggressive or demanding parents. Mrs. Winslow, however, applied the RAID Approach as a comprehensive preventive strategy.

The Approach's set format prevents overlooking valuable protective options and techniques. It should be emphasized that Mrs. Winslow chose options prior to her meeting with Mr. and Mrs. Morris. This is where the majority of school personnel err, because they wait until after contact with the parent has been made before using valuable options.

Mr. Brown, who incorporated the first two steps of the RAID Approach, was also proactive in that he realized that his emotional state might possibly interfere with his ability to interact with Mrs. Cananski.

As evident in these scenarios, the RAID Approach is easy to apply. No advanced counseling skills are necessary, and all of the steps are constructed with the staff member's protection in mind. Like any technique or method, the RAID Approach becomes easier with practice. It certainly doesn't take long to master, and the benefits of it greatly outweigh the short period of time necessary to become acquainted with its brief but simple steps.

QUESTIONS FOR DISCUSSION

1. Have you ever encountered parents similar to Mr. and Mrs. Morris or Mrs. Cananski? What were the results of these interactions? Did you consider the interactions positive or negative?

2. Of all the options and techniques employed by Mrs. Winslow and Mr. Brown, which ones would have been the most difficult for you to perform? For example, could you have set parameters and informed Mr. Morris that his comments would not be tolerated?

3. Do you consider the RAID Approach a practical way to engage confrontational or aggressive parents? How does this approach differ from your usual manner of interaction with this type of parent(s)?

PART III

Issues, Questions, and Installation

CHAPTER TEN

The Worst-Case Scenario . . . and After

Thus far, I have illustrated situations in which the RAID Approach has effectively remediated the situation at hand. But what happens if the unexpected occurs and an interaction turns violent or overly confrontational? Employees cannot foretell, either realistically or consistently, the outcomes of their parental encounters. I liken this situation to an airline pilot who can inform his or her passengers that according to the plane's radar, skies look favorable for a smooth flight. Even with advanced forecasting instruments, turbulence might still be encountered during the flight. Similarly, as it relates to aggression on school campuses, no technique or approach can be 100% effective regarding the prevention of encounters with aggressive individuals. Whenever school personnel are involved in sensitive, highly charged situations, the emergence of a problem remains a very real possibility.

During the past several years, I've met a superintendent who was shot in the head with a rifle and learned of another who was actually kidnapped from his office. One superintendent was tragically murdered at his job site, and I learned of a teacher who was severely injured when a parent entered the school and assaulted her because of a simple issue that could have easily been resolved. Fortunately, tragedies of these magnitudes don't occur frequently; nevertheless, there are countless situations where school personnel are accosted in some way. However, these situations don't garner the media attention that the aforementioned incidences do.

When a parent becomes aggressive or overly confrontational, what is the most advisable course of action for school personnel? I suppose this depends on the type of aggression being perpetrated. For instance, a school nurse might be blocked from exiting her office, or a school social worker might be verbally threatened. A teacher has his personal space invaded, or a principal has her name plaque thrown at her. A front-office worker is the recipient of an obscene gesture, or a guidance counselor in her office—without a colleague in the vicinity—is shoved by a parent. It becomes obvious that different levels of aggression require different responses by school personnel.

I could reason that, if implemented properly, the RAID Approach might prevent some of the previously mentioned situations. For example, could the nurse be blocked from exiting her office if she was seated in close proximity to the door? Could a name plate be thrown at a principal if all weapon-like objects had already been removed from her desk? Would the guidance counselor be without necessary support if she had prearranged for a colleague to also attend the meeting? Although the RAID Approach might preclude some situations, no method guarantees that aggression will never occur.

It goes beyond the scope of this book to discuss a response to every violent situation, but I would like to briefly mention several general techniques that might assist school personnel if they are physically confronted. According to former police officer and physical intervention expert Joone Kim (2003) in *Campus Safety Journal*,

Comprehensive training begins with basics such as enhancing one's awareness of possible threats and acting proactively to decrease the chances of becoming a victim. Awareness is more than just looking around. It is a proactive mindset that involves educated observation and effective response. The unfortunate truth is that in many cases of violence, there were warning signs and windows of opportunity where violence would have been averted. This is why it's important to learn what to look for and what preventative measures to take. (p. 12)

Regarding the unpredictability of aggression, Kim explained,

Violence by its very nature is unpredictable. Even when we educate ourselves to recognize potential threats, it is usually impossible to know when violence will strike. In order to react safely and effectively, the staff should receive training on basic physical techniques they can use to defend themselves and help others. They need to know what to expect and how to react. Anyone who has been involved in a physical altercation for the first time knows the actual experience is nothing like what they thought it would be. (p. 12)

Kim also provides several practical tips if school personnel become engaged in a violent encounter:

1. People tend to close their eyes when they think they're going to be hit. By fighting the urge to close their eyes, school personnel can become aware of what is transpiring and then react more effectively.

2. Watch the aggressor's hands. They can be used as weapons, and they also hold weapons. Do something. Scream, kick, or run. The worst thing to do is to do nothing. Avoid letting the shock of the situation freeze you. Doing something does not always constitute physical activity. Whether talking to the aggressor, contacting the police, or evacuating bystanders, something can always be done to address the situation.

3. When attacked, it's easy to panic, have tunnel vision, and subsequently focus only on what is in front of you. Therefore, try to have presence of mind. Subsequently, you are able to make decisions and act accordingly. Look for opportunities for escape or devise ways to outwit the assailant.

4. Don't turn your back to the aggressor unless there is an opportunity to run away. Maintain a will to survive, and do not give up. People who have survived difficult situations aren't superhuman, they simply refused to give up.

These tips can guide school personnel during encounters with aggressive individuals, but it's also a frightening thought that these tips might actually have to be implemented. When school personnel enter the field of education, violent interactions are not usually considered, because few people think that education includes placing themselves in dangerous situations. As a result, school personnel are usually ill prepared for these situations, at least in the formal sense. Realistically, however, hostile encounters should be considered a possibility no matter how remote the chances of occurrence. Although they remain difficult to predict, violent reactions necessitate a certain level of awareness and preparation by school personnel.

The following Web sites contain valuable information and options regarding personal safety during an actual physical assault:

Self defense now.com/

Protective Strategies.com/components.html

Kidpower.org/articles/safety-tips.html

Busseystyle.com/resources/article-8 tips.shtml

AFTER THE CONFRONTATION

Try to recall a simple disagreement with a friend or acquaintance when words were exchanged. Whether you considered yourself the winner or the loser in this minor conflict, it was probably still emotionally upsetting when you later sat down and thought about the situation and attempted to regain your composure. Now, try to imagine a verbal encounter with a stranger in a grocery store parking lot. The period it now takes to regain your composure might take much longer. Certainly, it's emotionally rattling to most people when they become verbally involved in a confrontation with a stranger or an acquaintance. If the confrontation is physical in nature, more severe psychological repercussions might result.

After an unpleasant encounter, a staff member should have an opportunity to discuss the experience. It's imperative that school personnel not be left to their own devices to deal with these situations. So often, an individual's involvement in a turbulent encounter and the consequent effects go unattended, because, as discussed in Chapter 1, school personnel might feel that it is their sole responsibility to deal with the parent. Unfortunately, this view is potentially damaging to the staff member.

I GOTTA UNLOAD: THE
IMPORTANCE OF DEBRIEFING

Have you ever watched a TV war documentary and noted the soldiers' faces after they engaged in a fierce battle? Their expressions usually seem blank, confused, and scared. The soldiers seem to be asking, "What just happened to me?" Maybe the violence they experienced occurred before they even knew what was in store for them. I often wonder if, after the battle, these brave people had any opportunity to vent their emotions in a structured, therapeutic manner. Unfortunately, from the veterans with whom I've spoken, the opportunity simply was not always available. The only option was to carry on, because it was their job to do so. Sadly, we have all heard stories of our veterans returning home and experiencing psychological repercussions because of their involvement in difficult situations.

Fortunately, through the years, many professions, including the military, have grown more sensitive to the negative repercussions from trauma. Police officers, fire fighters, and EMS workers now have the opportunity or are actually mandated to psychologically debrief after engaging in duties that involve severe violence, accidents, or catastrophes. Recently, the events of September 11, 2001, resulted in rescue personnel participating in these structured debriefing programs. Military personnel now also debrief as part of their activities. We have come a long way toward more adequately addressing the mental health concerns of professionals as they engage in traumatic duties.

School personnel are no different from other professionals who engage in distressing duties. After a highly emotional encounter, certain tasks might help to ensure their psychological well-being. I recommend that immediately after an altercation with a parent, staff members go to a room alone, attempt to sort out what happened, and at least try to relax. Also, I think it's a good idea to jot down the events and concerns that emerged during the encounter, because these facts might not be recalled later in the day. Next, and most importantly, school personnel should have the opportunity to discuss the incident and relate their feelings and experiences regarding the incident. Unfortunately, many professionals fail to take advantage of this opportunity when it is available. Several reasons for this failure might include the excessive time and effort it takes to discuss the event, the staff member's perception that no one really wants to discuss the situation, or the staff member's refusal to admit that the encounter with the parent had any effect on him or her. However, these reasons are erroneous.

First, discussing participation in a confrontation or altercation does not need to take a long period of time. A short and informal meeting, a debriefing of sorts, might occur with a coworker (e.g., a school administrator). More formal meetings may be sought if the staff member's reactions necessitate options other than those that school personnel can provide (e.g., a referral for community mental health counseling).

Second, the staff member's perception that no one cares to discuss the event with him or her might be real if this opportunity has not been a part of the school's regular procedure. If school personnel are provided the opportunity and made aware of the availability of informal discussions related to turbulent events, their willingness to participate in these meetings might increase.

Third, I've observed many colleagues respond to school crises and subsequently refuse to participate in informal, postcrisis discussion. They refuse to acknowledge that the situation and its residual stress might have had any effect on them. Unfortunately, several forms of stress might affect school personnel as a result of their interactions with aggressive or hostile individuals. These forms of stress can be cognitive, emotional, physical, or social/behavioral in nature.

According to Mitchell and Everly (1995), the cognitive effects of stress include decision-making difficulties, confusion, a decrease in higher cognitive functioning, and lowered concentration. All of these traits are imperative if school personnel are to function adequately in the school setting. Some of the emotional effects of stress might include feelings of anger, shock, disbelief, or depression. Often, these emotions need to be expressed in order for staff members to realize that their reactions and feelings are usually normal. In addition, the physical effects of stress might result in physical ailments. I have conversed with school personnel who experienced stomach disorders, insomnia, hypertension, teeth grinding, headaches, and an assortment of other health-related difficulties. Finally, the social/behavioral effects of stress might result in increased sensitivity to criticism, withdrawal from colleagues, lack of patience, or even a loss of appetite. Resource A provides a checklist that gauges an individual's stress reaction to a trauma.

SUMMARY

The RAID Approach helps to ensure that school personnel take precautions regarding parental aggression, although they still might experience aggression or hostility with little forewarning. Although usually not accustomed to functioning in these situations, school personnel can apply easy and practical techniques that might decrease the likelihood of harm. After enduring the discomfort of the turbulent encounter with the parent, school personnel should always have the opportunity to engage in a short, informal debriefing session of sorts. These debriefing sessions allow staff members to address the cognitive, emotional, physical, and social/behavioral effects of stress. Although school personnel might neglect this activity for several reasons, its importance should never be overlooked.

QUESTIONS FOR DISCUSSION

1. In the academic setting, have you ever encountered a person whom you felt intended to harm you? What was your reaction?

2. After you were informed of or witnessed a colleague experiencing a turbulent encounter, did he or she need to talk to someone about the incident? Do you feel that this colleague should have discussed the incident with someone?

3. After school personnel encounter an aggressive or hostile parent, do you feel that there is value in informal debriefing sessions?

CHAPTER ELEVEN

Four Great Questions

Throughout my research and many presentations on the RAID Approach, I've noted that certain questions consistently emerged. As a result, in this chapter, I decided to include four of the most frequently asked questions and my responses.

WHAT IF A PARENT BECOMES AGGRESSIVE AND A STUDENT IS IN THE VICINITY?

When posed with this question, I immediately recalled instances when this occurred. At the time, these students were simply working as front-office assistants or innocently passing through a front-office area. Because parents occasionally arrive unexpectedly on campus, this affords school personnel little time to prepare for their arrival. Sometimes, an angered parent might not even make his or her first contact with a staff member, but rather a student, and this is unfortunate because a student should never be exposed to an adult's inappropriate behavior in the scholastic setting.

What is the best course of action when a parent is displaying aggressive behavior in the presence of a student? Because every school makes student safety a priority, I recommend that if a conflict emerges, the staff member send the student, at once, to a specified location away from the parent. For example, after the parent's behavior becomes an obvious concern, a front-office worker might firmly state, "Millie, would you please go to the guidance office (or some other location) now." No reason for this request needs to be given to the student, because it is critical that he or she immediately exit the proximity of the parent. At the time, this request may seem odd to the student; however, explanations can be provided later. Although this option might seem to be mere common sense, students unfortunately continue to remain exposed to volatile interactions between school staff and parents. The rule of thumb is that if there is even a remote chance that a problem might arise with a parent, remove the student from the vicinity as quickly as possible.

This situation leads to another question: What if the child cannot be removed in time and is exposed to hostile behaviors? I could best answer this question by asking a staff member if he or she has ever witnessed or been personally involved in a highly charged situation on a school campus. Chances are, other people were in the vicinity, and it's easily conceivable that one of the witnesses to this encounter might have been a student. Although the staff member may have been slightly unnerved as a result of the incident, he or she also had the opportunity to discuss the situation and possibly vent his or her emotions to a colleague or staff member. This is a wise and healthy option, but is the same option available for a student after he or she witnesses a volatile situation? In the encounters that I personally recalled between parents and staff members, the students, unfortunately, were not attended to after the incident. It seems that in the aftermath of the situation, the possible effects of the confrontation on the student were unintentionally overlooked. In much the same way that school personnel might experience adverse psychological effects after a volatile encounter, it's logical that students might also experience these effects.

I recommend that after a student witnesses a volatile situation between a staff member(s) and parent, he or she should have the opportunity to discuss the situation. The most appropriate staff member to engage the student would be a school guidance counselor, but regardless, some type of staff member should always discuss the incident with the student(s) who witnessed the incident. Similar to an adult staff member, if the student experiences repercussions that require assistance beyond the scope of school personnel, options outside of the school might be considered. Finally, if a student witnesses, or is in any way involved in, an unpleasant experience between a parent and staff member, his or her parents and teacher should be notified, because the student's behavior could be affected by the incident.

What If a Parent Confronts a Staff Member Off Campus?

Every educator has seen one of his or her students or one of the student's family members outside of the school setting. For the most part, conversations are pleasant and brief, and staff members and family members bid each other farewell without incident. Conversely, seeing a parent with whom you've had a difficult experience is an altogether different situation. These contacts can be downright scary. But why? First, I think that one of the overlooked benefits of a school campus is the presence of colleagues who can afford protection or support if necessary during encounters with aggressive individuals. These coworkers are obviously not available after school or on a weekend while the staff member is shopping in a supermarket or video store where a parent might also be at the time.

What does a school employee do during these situations? I think this depends on the nature of the previous encounter. If a parent has made overt threats toward the staff member at school, then avoidance might be the best course of action. If the parent is in Aisle 3, stay in Aisle 6. Better yet, leave the store and shop later. Understandably, school personnel might ask, "Why should I have to change my lifestyle because of a parent?" I totally agree with this sentiment; however, a parent who could conceivably inflict harm should be avoided until support is available. For example, if the staff member decides to stay and shop, he or she should consider remaining in close proximity to the store's security officer in case the parent becomes aggressive. Also, when the staff member exits the store, he or she should remain aware of parking lots where other employees or protection are not available. These are easy locations for unwanted confrontations.

If the nature of the conflict does not warrant an immediate exit from a specific location, and the staff member cannot avoid interacting with the parent, a conversation might be unavoidable. Although not a dangerous situation, these interactions can be uncomfortable for both parties. I think it would be wise to use techniques contained in Step Four of the RAID Approach. We discussed how to approach the parent, observe them, make good eye contact, smile, greet them by name, and try to diffuse their anger. After implementing these simple tasks, try to keep the conversation light. Avoid discussion related to the original conflict. Unfortunately, parents might feel compelled to bring up the issue. For example, the comment, "I know we've had our problems, but I still think that Paul really didn't deserve a C in your class," might put the staff member in an uncomfortable position. An appropriate, nonconfrontational response might be, "I'm glad we had the opportunity to discuss that last week. If you feel that we need to discuss it again, just call for an appointment. I'd be glad to meet with you." Try not to elaborate on the issue, and attempt to direct attention to a safe topic. For instance, "These prices are getting so expensive!" Look for an opportunity to terminate the conversation when the opportunity becomes available.

Which Staff Member Plays the Most Important Role in the RAID Approach?

I've emphasized throughout this book that the RAID Approach is a multidisciplinary endeavor whose goal is the prevention of parental aggression in the scholastic setting. For it to be implemented successfully, however, the entire school staff must first take an interest in the approach. Numerous examples have been offered that illustrated the involvement of various types of school personnel during a colleague's encounter with an aggressive parent. Similar to the importance of every member of a football team, every staff member is important in the effective implementation of the RAID Approach. Football teams do, however, have two members who tend to assume larger roles in the team's success—the head coach and the quarterback. Similarly, two types of school personnel assume critical roles regarding the administration of the RAID Approach—school administrators and front-office workers/secretaries.

Throughout my years as a school social worker, I've noted a strong correlation between the staff's perception of the importance of an issue and the degree to which school administrators promote a specific issue. For instance, if a principal announces that improved attendance is a priority for the upcoming school year and periodically reaffirms his or her commitment to this effort, chances are, his or her staff will make efforts to improve attendance in a variety of ways. If the administration informs school personnel that reading performance must improve and that new and innovative programs will be implemented, the staff will likely consider this effort important.

In much the same way, if administrators convey to their employees that the issue of parental aggression is significant and should be addressed via a schoolwide, multidisciplinary approach, the staff will probably recognize this effort as worthwhile. School administrators are wonderful at selling ideas to their staffs. Their enthusiasm and commitment can definitely increase the overall acceptance of the RAID Approach and its effectiveness.

Another type of staff member who plays a critical role in the success of the RAID Approach is the front-office worker, including secretaries. Unfortunately, these employees are often overlooked in their efforts involving aggressive individuals. Front-office personnel usually have the first contact with aggressive or confrontational parents. Whether on the telephone or in person, front-office workers are in an advantageous position to observe and gauge a parent's level of aggression. This task is important because it dictates the method by which school personnel will subsequently interact with the parent. For example, a parent arrives at the front office and angrily demands to see the school social worker. According to the RAID Approach, the front-office worker should walk to the school social worker's location and inform him or her of the parent's arrival and demeanor. At that time, the school social worker can proceed with the RAID Approach, or, if the parent is intensely angry, he or she might refuse to meet with the parent. In addition, front-office workers can evacuate students from the vicinity of the angry parent. As discussed in Chapter 7, front-office workers/secretaries can also act as interveners when they intentionally interrupt meetings between staff members and parents. As you might recall, this task provides their colleagues with an opportunity to receive support from other personnel if their meeting with the parent turns volatile. Front-office workers and secretaries are truly key figures in the interactions that their colleagues might have with aggressive individuals.

How Do You Handle a Parent When He or She Returns to the School?

It's interesting how one or two unpleasant interactions with school personnel might result in the parent establishing a poor reputation at the school. I can easily imagine several staff members standing in a front-office area noting the oncoming approach of a troublesome parent, and someone commenting, "Batten down the hatches, here comes Mrs. Ingle." After a turbulent encounter with a parent, school personnel can be assured that at some point in the future, the parent will return to the school for another matter. During these return visits, staff members understandably might be uncomfortable or at least cautiously aware of the parent's presence. One educator suggested to me that a list might help inform front-office personnel of the identity of troublesome parents.

Is there a preferred course of action when a troublesome parent revisits a school? Should there even be a course of action for these individuals, or should "bygones be bygones"? As you can tell by now, I am a firm believer in prevention when it pertains to aggression. Therefore, I would recommend having an established approach available when the parent revisits campus. For example, in September, the RAID Approach worked very well with Mr. Johnson when he came to school and demanded to see the guidance counselor. What does the same guidance counselor do when the father—although much more composed—revisits the school several months later? Several advantages now exist for school personnel that weren't available prior to their previous meeting with the parent.

First, school personnel now possess a heightened sense of awareness regarding Mr. Johnson's potential to become volatile. This sense of awareness might not have existed before.

Second, the counselor is cognizant of the parent's capacity to emotionally provoke her. This information is invaluable because she is now aware of Mr. Johnson's manner of operation, and, to an extent, the staff can be prepared for his behavior.

Third, the counselor might review what advantages were effective during the previous encounter with Mr. Johnson. For example, was a colleague present during the meeting? Was the venue appropriate? The guidance counselor might reconsider any advantage that she implemented previously, and reuse it if she feels it might prove to be effective again.

Finally, when approaching and initially contacting Mr. Johnson, the same techniques might be considered, including close observation, a confident appearance, and a warm greeting. As the meeting commences, however, the staff member should be firm that a repeat of the aggression will not be tolerated. If Mr. Johnson's behavior previously necessitated the presence of law enforcement or administrative personnel, it might be in the guidance counselor's best interest to again make these personnel available.

Under no circumstance should an unprepared staff member attempt to meet with a parent who has previously exhibited aggressive, overly confrontational behavior. A certain amount of caution and planned options or alternatives can only act as a safeguard for further acts of aggression on the parent's behalf. The best course of action might be to review the effects of the RAID Approach during the previous interaction with the parent and note the most effective techniques and options used during that encounter.

QUESTIONS FOR DISCUSSION

1. How motivated would your school be regarding the implementation of the RAID Approach? What obstacles might emerge regarding its implementation? How could these obstacles be overcome?

2. School administrators and front-office personnel assume major roles in the successful implementation of the RAID Approach. Do you feel that other staff members also might play large roles in the approach?

3. Have you ever had an interaction with a parent after he or she had previously presented difficulties? What were your feelings regarding the second encounter?

4. If a parent's previous behavior made you wary of him or her for the second encounter, would you avoid the parent? What would be your option(s)?

Resource A

*Traumatic Stress
Reactions Questionnaire*

1. Have you experienced, witnessed, or been confronted with an event that involved actual or threatened death, serious injury, or threat of death or injury and responded with feelings of fear, helplessness, or horror?
Yes O No O

Have you ever persistently experienced

2. recurrent and intrusive recollections of the event that are distressing?
Yes O No O

3. recurrent and distressing dreams/nightmares of the event?
Yes O No O

4. feeling like or acting as if the traumatic event was happening again or having flashbacks or other sensory experiences of reliving the event?
Yes O No O

5. feeling very distressed when you experience internal or external cues that remind you of the traumatic event?
Yes O No O

6. having a physical response (e.g., increased heart rate, nausea, etc.) when you experience internal or external cues that remind you of the traumatic event?
Yes O No O

7. avoidance of feelings of numbness around stimuli associated with the traumatic event that may include
   - efforts to avoid thoughts, conversations, or feelings related to the trauma
   - avoidance of activities, places, or people who remind you of the trauma
   - forgetting important aspects of the traumatic events
   - having a loss of interest in important activities
   - feeling distant from others
   - having a restricted range of numbness of feelings/emotions
   - a sense that the future is threatened and possibly fore-shortened?
   Yes O No O

8. feeling an increased sense of tension/arousal that may be indicated by
   - difficulty falling or staying asleep
   - feeling irritable and/or having outbursts of anger
   - having difficulty concentrating
   - being easily startled
   - being hypervigilant (observing the environment so as to constantly notice impending threats)
   Yes O No O

Score Questionnaire

For this questionnaire, give yourself 1 point for every "yes" answer and 0 points for every "no" answer. Score: _____
So . . . is your score 4 or greater?

If you have been exhibiting four or more of these symptoms, you may want to find someone to talk to about the possibility that you are experiencing a significant stress reaction to a trauma.

If you or someone you know has frequent thoughts of death or suicide, seek professional help immediately.

Remember, a high score on this questionnaire does not necessarily mean you have a posttraumatic stress disorder—only an evaluation by an experienced clinician can make this determination.

Source: Adapted from the *Diagnostic and Statistical Manual of Mental Disorders, Fourth Edition, Text Revision* (American Psychiatric Association, 2002).

References

American Psychiatric Association. (2002). *Diagnostic and statistical manual of mental disorders, fourth edition, text revision.* Washington, DC: Author.

Blauvelt, P. (2001). *Inside School Safety: Effective Management Strategies for School Administrators, 6*(2), 1–12.

Brandt, R. (1998). Engaging parents and the community in schools. *Educational Leadership, 55*(8), 1–7.

Education Commission of the United States. (1966). *Listen, discuss and act.* Denver, CO: Author.

Jaksec, C. M. (2003). *The confrontational parent: A practical guide for school leaders.* Larchmont, NY: Eye On Education.

Kim, J. (2003). 6 things to do during a violent confrontation. *Campus Safety Journal, 11*(1), 12–13.

Lindle, J. (1989). What do parents want from principals and teachers? *Educational Leadership, 47*(2), 12–14.

Margolis, H. (1990). What to do when you're verbally attacked: The critical moment. *NASSP Bulletin, 74*(523), 34–38.

Margolis, H., & Tewell, K. J. (1988). Resolving conflict with parents: A guide for administrators. *NASSP Bulletin, 72*(506), 1–8.

McEwan, E. K. (1998). *How to deal with parents who are angry, troubled, afraid, or just plain crazy.* Thousand Oaks, CA: Corwin.

Mitchell, J. T., & Everly, G. S. (1995). *Critical incident stress debriefing: An operations manual for the prevention of trauma among emergency service and disaster workers* (2nd ed.). Baltimore: Chevron.

Storey, V. J. (1990). *Parent-school conflict: An exploratory study. Report of a research study.* (ERIC Document Reproduction Service No. ED 342109)

Whitaker, T., & Fiore, D. J. (2001). *Dealing with difficult parents (and with parents in difficult situations).* Larchmont, NY: Eye On Education.

Facilitator's Guide

WHO SHOULD USE THIS GUIDE?

The facilitator's guide for *The Difficult Parent: An Educator's Guide to Handling Aggressive Behavior* is designed for implementation by the following individuals and groups:

- School personnel who wish to introduce an approach that enables their colleagues to interact more effectively with aggressive or confrontational parents
- Principals who wish to install a preventive approach to parental aggression within their schools
- Superintendents who want to introduce the topic of parental aggression and its prevention to school district administrators

WHO SHOULD RECEIVE A "RAID APPROACH" IN-SERVICE?

If a staff member engages in any form of interaction with a parent, the possibility of a turbulent encounter exists. Because the RAID Approach is multidisciplinary in nature, all staff members should have the opportunity to benefit from the in-service. Possible participants include

- Superintendents
- District-level administrators
- Principals
- Assistant principals
- Teachers
- School social workers

- School psychologists
- Guidance counselors
- School nurses
- Front-office workers/secretaries
- Lunchroom personnel
- School resource officers

WHEN SHOULD THE RAID APPROACH BE INSTALLED?

Ideally, the RAID Approach should be installed at the beginning of the school year, because the earlier the approach is installed, the sooner school personnel can learn to interact more safely with parents. If an in-service program prior to the start of the school year is not possible, the RAID Approach can be installed at any time during the school year. I recommend, however, that once installed, the RAID Approach should be reviewed during the course of the school year. This refresher—which serves to review roles, responsibilities, successes, and complications—can be conducted most practically during staff meetings or professional days.

HOW THIS GUIDE IS ORGANIZED

This guide contains three modules, and several tasks are contained within each module. Also, a discussion question is included after each module. At the end of each module, a facilitator checklist ensures that important facets of the module have been addressed.

Module One is an introductory examination of the issue of parental aggression toward school personnel. Module Two explains the four steps of the RAID Approach, and Module Three allows the facilitator to install the RAID Approach in his or her specific academic setting.

Your group meetings can be arranged several ways:

- Conduct a single 1-hour session using only Modules Two and Three.
- Conduct two 1-hour sessions using all three modules.
- Select a specific module for review on a later date after the original in-service has been implemented.

WHAT MATERIALS ARE NECESSARY?

Materials for Facilitators

Copy of *The Difficult Parent: An Educator's Guide to Handling Aggressive Behavior*

Chart paper and markers

Overhead projector

Copies of exhibits from each module

Materials for Participants

Copies of *The Difficult Parent: An Educator's Guide to Handling Aggressive Behavior*

Paper and writing instruments for note-taking

MODULE ONE

Task One: Introduce the Issue of Parental Aggression

(Overheads # 1 and #2)

The facilitator's task is to introduce, then emphasize, the importance of the issue of parental aggression toward school personnel. Statistics, as contained in Chapters 1 and 2, should be used to reinforce this effort. The frequency and types of parental aggression should also be discussed. The facilitator might also note the relative obscurity of the issue and relative absence of information on the topic.

Discussion questions: Prior to this meeting, have any of you been aware of the issue of parental aggression? How and where were you made aware of this issue?

Facilitator Topic Checklist:

( ) Discuss the topic of school personnel and parental aggression (Overhead # 1).

( ) Discuss why the topic of parental aggression toward school personnel is obscure? (e.g., responsibility, resiliency, lack of awareness).

( ) Present and discuss parental aggression statistics (Overhead # 2).

Chapter 1 contains more information on these topics.

Task Two: Identification of Previous Staff Interactions With Aggressive Parents

Attempt to build a bridge between the topic of parental aggression and the staff's personal experiences with it. For instance, allow the staff an opportunity to describe their encounters with aggressive or confrontational parents.

Discussion questions: Have any of you interacted with an aggressive or confrontational parent? What was the reason for the difficulty?

Facilitator Topic Checklist:

( ) List the type of encounter in which the staff member was involved (chart paper).

( ) List the possible reason(s) for the difficulties during these encounters (chart paper).

( ) Discuss whether these encounters could have been avoided.

Chapter 3 contains more information on these topics.

Task Three: Identify the Possible Effects of Parental Aggression on School Personnel

(Overhead # 3)

The facilitator should describe the possible effects of parental aggression. The facilitator should also allow staff members to describe how they have been emotionally, socially, behaviorally, or physically affected by these interactions. The facilitator should closely monitor these voluntary disclosures in the event a staff member becomes overly emotional while discussing these repercussions.

Discussion questions: Has an encounter with an aggressive parent ever affected you in any way? What did you do to recover?

Facilitator Topic Checklist:

( ) Ask staff members to write a paragraph about their most volatile parental interaction. To ensure confidentiality, do not have staff sign their papers. Collect input.

( ) Choose several feedback papers and share these incidences with staff.

( ) Discuss the effects of staff encounters with volatile parents (Overhead # 2).

( ) List ways in which staff members recovered from these turbulent parental interactions (chart paper).

Chapter 1 contains more information on these topics.

Task Four: Establish the Value of a Multidisciplinary Approach to Parental Aggression

"The prevention of parental aggression is a schoolwide effort that will involve every staff member!" I suggest that the facilitator repeat this phrase at least five times during the in-service. The success of this effort is contingent on the staff's willingness to participate in its implementation. A schoolwide approach ensures that no staff member will have to endure an uncomfortable or dangerous encounter alone with a parent.

Discussion question: Can anyone identify a successful project or effort within this school that succeeded because of a schoolwide/ multidisciplinary approach?

Facilitator Topic Checklist:

( ) List projects within the school that have involved a multi-disciplinary approach (chart paper).

( ) On chart paper, write "Many hands make light work" and discuss this phrase's importance as it pertains to the application of a schoolwide approach to parental aggression.

Chapter 4 contains more information on these topics.

MODULE TWO

Task One: Introduce the RAID Approach

(Overheads # 4 and # 5)

School personnel greatly disdain complicated, time-absorbing procedures. With this in mind, the introduction to the actual steps of the RAID Approach should underscore its ease and practicality. It should also be emphasized that this approach is a preemptive strategy toward parental aggression. A great selling point is the fact that the RAID Approach can help school personnel avoid unpleasant parental encounters. It is not a reactive approach—in which the intention is to assist school personnel after a confrontation has begun—but a proactive approach to parental aggression.

Discussion questions: What are your thoughts about this proactive approach to parental aggression? How is this approach different from the way we have traditionally handled aggressive or confrontational parents?

Facilitator Topic Checklist:

( ) Discuss the school's traditional manner of dealing with aggressive parents (chart paper).

( ) Establish the need for a proactive versus a reactive approach to the problem of parental aggression.

( ) Introduce the RAID Approach (Overhead # 4).

( ) Discuss the features of the RAID Approach (Overhead # 5).

Chapter 4 contains more information on these topics.

Task Two: Explain Step One:
Recognizing the Potential for a Volatile Encounter

(Overhead # 6)

The facilitator might discuss the different strategies and school personnel roles contained in this important first step. For example, the facilitator can explain that front-office workers will now notify their colleagues face-to-face if a parent appears to be emotionally upset. It is also understood, however, that front-office workers will go directly to an administrator if the parent is excessively angry or is threatening. This is in contrast to the traditional way of notifying staff members by intercom of a parent's arrival.

The facilitator can explain the value of collecting information about the parent prior to actual contact (if a staff member suspects the parent of potentially being volatile). This brief but intentional hesitation is imperative because during this time, valuable information can be gathered about the parent and his or her past behaviors.

Another important discussion topic is the staff's decision to avoid interacting with an aggressive parent alone. The facilitator should reemphasize the RAID Approach's team design and also discuss a staff member's fear of asking a colleague for assistance. For example, the resource officer might inform the staff that he or she will be available if there is an encounter with a volatile parent. The facilitator could likewise confirm that the school administration is willing to immediately assist any staff member upon request. The facilitator should emphasize that it is better to be overly cautious than unprepared when engaging volatile parents.

Discussion question: Does delaying or hesitating before interacting with a parent differ from your traditional method of interaction?

Facilitator Topic Checklist:

Discuss the importance of

( ) Engaging the parent only after a brief delay

( ) Gathering information before engaging the parent

( ) Heeding warnings about meeting the parent

( ) Overcoming the urge to meet with a potentially volatile parent

( ) Postponing or rescheduling the meeting if the parent's behavior is a concern

( ) Informing an administrator (in person or in writing) of the postponement or rescheduling

Chapter 5 contains more information on these topics.

Task Three: Explain Step Two: Assessing Your Ability to Emotionally Handle the Situation

(Overhead # 7)

The facilitator can challenge school personnel to recall a time when personal issues may have affected their disposition at school. He or she should explain that a variety of personal or professional problems can easily affect any employee's mood or affect. Once this fact is identified, the facilitator can describe how a poor disposition or negative perception of the parent might negatively affect the interaction with the parent, who, coincidentally, might also be experiencing personal difficulties. Emphasis is placed on the importance of assessing emotional states *prior* to interactions with potentially volatile parents. The facilitator can also advise staff members that postponement or rescheduling is a viable option during these situations.

Discussion questions: Can you recall a time when your mood or affect might have interfered with your ability to interact effectively with a parent? What did you do? What was the outcome of the interaction?

Facilitator Topic Checklist:

Discuss the importance of

( ) Gaining an awareness of one's emotional state and negative perceptions of the parent(s)

( ) Establishing a stopping point if the staff member is experiencing a heightened state of emotions

( ) Having a colleague bring to a coworker's attention his or her bad mood or poor affect (prior to his or her interaction with a potentially volatile parent)

( ) Refusing to proceed with a meeting if heightened emotions or negative parental perceptions could interfere with the interaction

Chapter 6 contains more information on these topics.

Task Four: Explain Step Three: Identifying Your Advantages

(Overhead # 8)

This is an opportune time for staff members to collectively identify advantages that might allow them to interact more effectively and safely with aggressive or confrontational parents. These advantages are considered practical and easy to implement. For example, the facilitator might inform the staff that the presence of colleagues is a viable option when meeting with parents who are or might become volatile. Also, as previously discussed, using a "meeting interrupter," for the purposes of gauging the parent's anger, is another option. In addition, considerations such as the location of meetings, seating arrangements, and coverage for school personnel (usually for teachers) while meeting with parents can be addressed. It is also a good time to identify two rooms (in case one becomes unavailable) to be designated for use during parent/school personnel meetings.

Discussion question: Are there advantages within this school that we tend to overlook when interacting with aggressive parents?

Facilitator Topic Checklist:

Discuss the importance of accessing

( ) Workforce advantages—The identification of supportive colleagues who can also attend meetings with aggressive or confrontational parents

( ) Environmental advantages—The addition, subtraction, or manipulation of physical objects that might decrease the chance of aggressive behavior being directed toward school personnel

Room characteristics:

- Location (in proximity to other school personnel)
- Seating arrangement
- Visibility (proper lighting, open drapes and doors)
- Easy exits

Unique devices and considerations:

- Electronic devices
- Removal of objects that could be used as weapons

Chapter 7 contains more information on these topics.

Task Five: Explain Step Four: Diffusing Parent Anger During the Initial Approach and Greeting
(Overhead # 9)

Techniques included in this step can significantly affect interactions with parents. The facilitator can cover topics such as the importance of close observation, the physical approach to the parent, eye contact, facial expression, the initial greeting, and an invitation to discuss the issue at hand. In addition, meeting termination as the result of a parent's volatile behavior can also be discussed.

Discussion question: What do you feel is the most important technique for a staff member when he or she initially approaches a potentially aggressive parent? Eye contact? Handshake? Posture?

Facilitator Topic Checklist:

When approaching a potentially volatile parent, discuss the staff member's

( ) Eye contact

( ) Body posture

( ) Facial expression

( ) Voice tone/initial verbal greeting

Discuss the value of observing the parent's

( ) Behaviors

( ) Posture

( ) Voice tone/receptivity to greeting

Emphasize the importance of

( ) Terminating or rescheduling a meeting with a parent who is displaying problematic behavior

( ) Notifying an administrator of difficulties with an aggressive or confrontational parent and the choice to delay the meeting

Chapter 8 contains more information on these topics.

MODULE THREE

Task One: Solicit Feedback Regarding the RAID Approach

At this point in the in-service, the philosophy, framework, and operation of the RAID Approach have been made clear to the staff. The facilitator can now solicit feedback as an indicator of the staff's receptiveness to the RAID Approach. Responses to the staff's questions and comments should be straightforward. The overriding response theme is the fact that the RAID Approach is not a cure-all for aggression or hostility. Emphasize the approach's preemptive nature, which can help school personnel recognize and ultimately avoid turbulent encounters with parents.

Discussion questions: What are your feelings about the RAID Approach? Why do you think it can be effective and valuable in our school?

Facilitator Topic Checklist:

( ) Eliminate perception that the RAID Approach is a cure-all.

( ) Allow staff to voice their opinions regarding the RAID Approach.

( ) List opinions of the approach, and discuss concerns (e.g., lack of SRO, inadequate meeting locations, etc.) (chart paper).

( ) Reemphasize the importance of a schoolwide approach to parental aggression and the RAID Approach's role in this effort.

Task Two: Identify Roles and Responsibilities

On chart paper, the facilitator should briefly list school personnel and the roles they will assume in the RAID Approach. For example, the resource officer will be summoned to confront parents who display violent or threatening behaviors. The administration will address legal threats or actions, and front-office workers will be informers because they will notify their colleagues of an angry parent's arrival and disposition. A secretary might be assigned as the person who will intentionally interrupt staff/parent meetings in an effort to gauge the level of hostility. Any other designated roles can be illustrated and discussed at this time.

Discussion questions: Is anyone uneasy with his or her assignment in the RAID Approach? If so, how can it be altered to increase your comfort?

Facilitator Topic Checklist:

( ) List each type of staff member within the school and assign his or her role within the RAID Approach (chart paper). A handout containing assignments should be provided to staff members at a later date.

( ) Discuss the staff members' level of comfort in these roles, and modify roles and responsibilities if necessary.

Chapter 9 contains more information on these topics.

Task Three: Discuss Worst-Case Scenarios

The facilitator should be aware that some staff members might not consider their involvement in hostile/violent situations likely or even realistic. Regardless, it is still important to review the material found in Chapter 10 (Kim, 2003). The facilitator can emphasize that if even one staff member benefits from these techniques, the effort is worthwhile.

Discussion questions: Has anyone interacted with a parent who presented a safety concern (whether perceived or real) for you or a colleague? If so, how did you or your colleague react?

Facilitator Topic Checklist:

( ) Address violence awareness and the need for preparation.

( ) Discuss participant's involvement in violent encounters.

( ) Discuss practical tips for school personnel during violent confrontations. This information is found in Chapter 10 (handout or overhead).

Chapter 10 contains more information on these topics.

Task Four: Establish a Debriefing Mechanism

The debriefing effort does not need to be excessively formal in nature. It should be emphasized, however, that if a staff member engages in a turbulent encounter with a parent, another staff member will subsequently meet with that person to discuss his or her views or feelings regarding the situation. This intervention should be completed within a reasonable time span (e.g., 1 day). For example, if a school psychologist is physically threatened by a parent, the guidance counselor or administrator—on the day of the incident or the following school day—should take the opportunity to discuss the situation with his or her coworker. If the school psychologist suffers further repercussions from the incident, additional options (e.g., outpatient mental health counseling) could be explored.

The facilitator should explain that different staff members can provide this informal debriefing session. Principals, assistant principals, guidance counselors, the social workers, school nurses, or school psychologists can be identified as the best candidates to provide this valuable service. Members from district crisis intervention teams or community-based mental health personnel can also be debriefing designees.

If actual contact has occurred, the administrator and staff member may also want to review their district's policy regarding filing criminal charges against the parent.

Discussion questions: Would you be comfortable speaking with a colleague following a turbulent encounter with a parent? Do you feel that debriefing sessions are valuable?

Facilitator Topic Checklist:

( ) Discuss the importance of an informal debriefing session, which will be conducted after a violent encounter.

( ) Identify staff members who will actually conduct the debriefing sessions.

( ) Give a copy of Resource A, the Traumatic Stress Reactions Questionnaire, to all assigned debriefing personnel.

Chapter 10 contains more information on these topics.

SCHOOL PERSONNEL

AND

PARENTAL AGGRESSION

RESEARCH RESULTS

80% — *on 3 or more occasions,* **a threat was made to contact "other authorities"**

60% — *on 2 or more occasions,* **shouting or profanity was directed at the employee**

51% — *on 2 or more occasions,* **false accusations were leveled against the employee**

36% — **were present when a colleague was confronted by a parent**

27% — **experienced at least one incident of having their personal space invaded**

THE EFFECTS OF PARENTAL AGGRESSION

Cognitive

Emotional

Physical

Social

THE RAID APPROACH

Recognizing the potential for a volatile encounter

Assessing your ability to emotionally handle the situation

I dentifying your advantages

Diffusing the parent's aggression during the initial approach and greeting

---

RAID'S FEATURES

- Four simple steps

- Commonsense approach

- Based on school personnel's mistakes and successes

- Can be implemented in various situations

Step One

Recognize the potential for a volatile encounter

Step Two

Assess your ability to emotionally handle the situation

Step Three

Identify your advantages

Step Four

Diffuse the parent's aggression during the initial approach and greeting

Index

**CORWIN
PRESS**

The Corwin Press logo—a raven striding across an open book—represents the union of courage and learning. Corwin Press is committed to improving education for all learners by publishing books and other professional development resources for those serving the field of K–12 education. By providing practical, hands-on materials, Corwin Press continues to carry out the promise of its motto: **"Helping Educators Do Their Work Better."**